Jonathan Petre is the Edu   *y
Telegraph, having spent n   us
affairs.

After reading philosophy at Cambridge University, he joined the
Catholic Herald, the Roman Catholic weekly newspaper, where he
became news editor. In 1984, he moved to the Peterborough column
on the *Daily Telegraph* before becoming that newspaper's Religious
Affairs Correspondent. For three years he witnessed some of the
salient events of the women priests' debate – from the tragic
Crockford's affair to the consecration of Barbara Harris in Boston.
Between 1989 and 1993, when he took up his current post, he was a
political reporter at Westminster and a general news reporter.

He is married with two children and lives in South London.

BY SEX DIVIDED

The Church of England and Women Priests

by Jonathan Petre

To Emma

Fount
An Imprint of HarperCollins*Publishers*

Fount Paperbacks is an Imprint of
HarperCollins*Religious*
Part of HarperCollins*Publishers*
77–85 Fulham Palace Road, London W6 8JB

First published in Great Britain
in 1994 by Fount Paperbacks

1   3   5   7   9   10   8   6   4   2

A catalogue record for this book is
available from the British Library

ISBN 0 00 627816–7

Typeset by Harper Phototypesetters Limited,
Northampton, England
Printed and bound in Great Britain by
HarperCollinsManufacturing Glasgow

Contents

'There are three sexes – men, women and clergymen.'
THE REVD SYDNEY SMITH (1771–1845)

Preface

By the summer of 1994, more than 1,200 women had been ordained as priests in the Church of England, bringing to an end one of the most turbulent chapters in recent ecclesiastical history. Few issues have provoked such rancour and bitterness, division and dissent.

This book is a journalist's attempt to capture some of the flavour of these extraordinary times – from the early struggles of women to make their voices heard to the dramatic denouncement on 11 November 1992, and its aftermath. It has a global setting, and a cast of intriguing characters. It is not written by an insider, nor does it aspire to the heights of an academic treatise.

In writing it, however, I have been able to call on the observations of some of the leading protagonists, who have shed new light on the events. I am particularly indebted to those who gave up substantial amounts of time to talk to me. They include Dr Robert Runcie, his successor as Archbishop of Canterbury Dr George Carey, Dr Graham Leonard, Peter Geldard, George Austin, Diana McClatchey, and Joyce Bennett.

I also received invaluable assistance and advice from Brian Hanson, Ted Harrison (whose book *Much Beloved Daughter* contained fascinating detail about Tim Oi Li), the Movement for the Ordination of Women, Archbishop Robin Eames, John Broadhurst, John Taylor, Bishop of St Albans, Lesley Perry, the Archbishop of Canterbury's press officer, my wife for countless cups of coffee, and many others too numerous to mention. Any errors, infelicities or misjudgements are, of course, entirely my responsibility.

1

The Vote

The Revd Katharine Rumens had not expected such a good seat – or indeed any seat – for the debate. Along with hundreds of other women, she had congregated early outside Church House, the Church of England's ivy-veined nerve centre in the shadow of Westminster Abbey, prepared for an anxious wait in the autumnal gloom. The vote was not anticipated for another nine hours. Within minutes of her arrival, however, she learned that a fellow campaigner had queued since dawn to reserve a handful of the few remaining places in the public gallery – the balcony suspended over the circular debating chamber like the 'gods' in a theatre. From there, she could command a lofty view of the concentric rings of wooden benches seating the 574 men and women who were to determine their future.

Rumens had journeyed in on the Underground from the gritty East London parish where she served as a curate. One of 1,300 women deacons yearning for ordination to the priesthood, her clerical collar, black cassock and long silver earrings drew curious glances from the rush-hour passengers. On the steps of Church House, however, she was immediately at home, embracing friends and fellow campaigners, helping to distribute symbolic white flowers to new arrivals and encouraging impromptu hymn-singing to reinforce morale. Then she climbed up to the eyrie of the public gallery and took her seat.

Later, the television cameras would capture Rumens' expression of restrained euphoria mingled with incredulity and not a little relief as the result was announced. Despite the Archbishop of Canterbury's exhortation that the outcome be heard in silence, she could not contain a shriek of excitement which seemed to reverberate around the chamber. Reaching over to hug her friends, she hardly noticed the reproving stares.

Fr Peter Geldard had risen at 6 o'clock that morning to dress in sober clerical black and recite Holy Office. He had got to bed late, having spent the previous evening rallying fellow opponents of the women's ordination Measure. At a meeting of 180 members of the High Church Anglo-Catholic group in room 301, one of the numerous halls running off Church House's rabbit warren of corridors, the mood had been buoyant; the consensus was that the legislation would fail by a few votes. But Geldard, who as leader of the group had spent days pouring over the arithmetic permutations of the vote, privately harboured fears that it would squeeze through. For the sake of morale, he judged it unwise to share his doubts with his colleagues, but he was already preparing his ground; a victory for the legislation by one or two votes, he was saying, would hardly constitute a sufficient basis for change.

As he set off from his London lodgings later to attend the 7.30 a.m. mass at the Anglo-Catholic sanctum of St Matthew's, Westminster, he mentally rehearsed his speech, hoping that it could yet prove influential. Indeed afterwards, it was to be hailed as a *tour de force* and one of the few influential contributions to the debate – Geldard had delivered it without notes while glancing at a stop watch which allowed him to use all but two seconds of the ten minutes allotted him. But by the end of the day he would be signalling his intention to sever his links with the Church into which he had been ordained 22 years earlier and 'crossing the Tiber' into the Roman Catholic Church. In his speech, he had warned the Synod that by approving women priests, it would be 'pushing down one of the walls that hold the very house together'. All around him he could hear the rumble of collapsing masonry.

The date was 11 November 1992. After two decades of demonstrations and debates, vigils and petitions, floutings of the law and threats of schism, high principle and low cunning, even the suicide of an Oxford don, the Church of England had finally arrived at the moment of decision. The members of General Synod – its parliament – were wedged into their benches well before prayers at 10 a.m., the preliminary to what was to prove an emotive if sometimes curiously stilted debate. The subject on the agenda, item 502, was the Draft Priests (Ordination of Women) Measure. It was an extraordinary piece of legislation, a recipe for officially sanctioned division. Apart from permitting the ordination of women priests, it provided a complex framework of safeguards for those who, in conscience, could not accept such a departure from 450 years of Anglican history. The participants' awareness that the Church had reached a defining moment in its history was heightened by the presence of the television arc lights, which raised the temperature in the domed chamber and bathed the proceedings in an unearthly glare. The level of security was also unprecedented; all Synod members had been issued with identity cards which they were required to produce on request. After only a few minutes into the opening speech the fire alarm bells rang and the chamber had to be evacuated. Initial fears that a bomb had been planted in the building proved groundless; the cause was traced to a burning pan in the Italian restaurant downstairs, run, ironically, by a family of devout Roman Catholics. After a short adjournment, the Archbishop of York, Dr John Habgood, who was chairing the morning session, reopened the proceedings with the suggestion that the alarm, having proved false, should be regarded a good omen. Not all the signs were as auspicious.

Throughout the day, the sense of division within the ranks of a Church which proclaims unity from its pulpits was palpable. Supporters and opponents could barely speak to each other. In a room in Methodist Central Hall across the road from Church House, members of the Movement for the Ordination of Women (MOW), the pressure group which had done more than any other to promote the female cause, gathered around a television to watch the BBC's live coverage of the debate. The near reverential hush was punctuated with cheers for speakers who favoured the Measure, while threats of resignation from die-hard opponents were met with uncharitable calls of 'Bye, bye'. As the time of the vote approached, the room gradually emptied as its occupants went to swell the ranks staging a candle-light vigil in Dean's Yard, the square of grass outside Church House.

Dr George Carey, who was chairing the afternoon session, had more at stake than most. That morning, he had effectively risked his authority as Archbishop of Canterbury by delivering an unexpectedly firm partisan speech in favour of women priests. He had told the Synod: 'God calls us to take the risk of faith. I believe that God is also calling his Church to ordain women to the priesthood.' It was a typically forthright gamble, and, in restrospect, critical, though the mood at lunch among supporters of the Measure, including the members of the steering committee, was despondent. Geldard's portrayal of the legislation, in which he painted a disturbing picture of diocese pitched against diocese, parish against parish, had made an impact. If the vote went the wrong way, the Archbishop would end up looking distinctly foolish. He had spent long hours bent over his word processor in his gloomy study at Lambeth Palace agonizing over the tone of the speech. While many had pressed him to adopt a neutral, statesmanlike stance, allowing him maximum room for manoeuvre whatever the outcome of the vote, he had decided to lead from the front. 'I remember Graham James, my chaplain, coming in when I had just completed the first draft,' recalls Carey. 'He said to me, "this could be the most important speech of your archipiscopate" and I remember that I was very surprised. But I began to think, yes, he is probably right about that, and it made it more urgent to get it right. So it was knocked around quite a bit. I checked with people that the tone was right. It was quite painstaking and very careful.'

So it was with some trepidation that, at 4.40p.m., after five hours of debate and some forty speeches – many of them retreading the inconclusive theological routes so often explored in the Synod – he called on its members to stand and be counted. Such was the sensitivity of the moment that, over previous weeks, the Synod's bewigged legal advisor Brian Hanson had been urged to replace his normal cry of 'Divide' with the less adversarial 'Decide', an innovation he resisted. After rising from their seats and bowing their heads in a moment of silent prayer, clergy and lay Synod members excitedly filed towards four doors, two marked Ayes and two Noes.

The bishops moved towards the centrally positioned chairman's platform, with those in favour gathering on the right hand of the Archbishop, those against on his left. Fifteen minutes later, when everyone had regained their seats and the hubbub had subsided, Dr Carey was handed a piece of paper and, in a slightly quavering voice, he announced the result: House of Bishops: ayes 39, noes 13; House of Clergy: ayes 176, noes 74; House of Laity: ayes 169, noes 82.

The mathematics took a second to sink in. By the required two-thirds majority in each House, the General Synod had given its blessing to the greatest upheaval in the Church's history, but the result could hardly have been closer. Thirteen bishops had voted against, and one had abstained. The narrowest margin was recorded, as expected, in the House of Laity, where 82 (32.7 per cent) members were against. If that figure had been 84, the legislation would have been defeated, even though the overall proportion in all three Houses together would still have been more than two to one. Observers recall that one of the female members of the House of Laity had remained rooted in her seat when the ballot was called, apparently in floods of tears. The wife of an Anglo-Catholic priest, she had been elected to the Synod by the Oxford diocese on a negative ticket, but, when the moment came, was unable to bring herself to cast her vote against the Measure. They also saw Sir John Owen, the Dean of Arches (the senior ecclesiastical judge), break his normal practice of abstaining in debates to cast his vote, reputedly in favour. 'That's how close things were,' one said later.

While the mood of the debate might have appeared to swing first one way and then the other – most markedly during the contributions of Carey and Geldard – in reality the vast majority knew in advance where their allegiances would ultimately lie. The critical sea-change had occurred in the days and weeks preceding the debate, when both sides had employed robust lobbying tactics more appropriate to a Parliamentary whips office than a body of Christians claiming the guidance of the Holy Spirit. 'We used every trick in the book,' commented one activist. 'The whips could learn a thing or two from us.' Just four months earlier, a victory for supporters of women priests had appeared tantalizingly out of reach. At the July meeting of the General Synod in York – in what was seen as a dry run for the autumn vote – a simple majority in all Houses was needed to bring the Measure before the November Synod for final approval. The result of the voting in the House of Laity – 148 (61.41 per cent) in favour to 93 (38.59 per cent) against – caused a panic in the pro-ordination lobby. Though sufficient on this occasion, the result fell below the two-thirds threshold that would be required in November. Supporters of women priests calculated that, if the figures were replicated in four months time, the Measure would fall by 13 votes.

A period of feverish activity followed. While opponents of the Measure concentrated on consolidating their position, supporters targeted known waverers, the majority of whom were in the evangelical camp, bombarding them with leaflets and 'friendly' visits. The atmosphere was further soured as stories circulated that women deacons were being denounced as 'white witches' and hissed by opponents in certain Anglo-Catholic churches, and even barred from the sanctuary. On the eve of the debate, the corridors and tea rooms of Church House resembled the lobbies of the House of Commons before a crucial vote; small groups plotted in every corner, tension hung in the air. In the coffee queues, no one was allowed to stand alone too long; some voters found themselves being lobbied simultaneously by activists from both sides. The outcome was so finely balanced – an eve-of-debate BBC opinion poll predicted that the Measure would fail by less than one per cent of the vote in the House of Laity – that ailing and elderly Synod members were urged to vote at all costs. At the eleventh hour, supporters gained a prominent scalp when Mark Birchall, the lay chairman of the influential Evangelical group in Synod, declared that he would vote for the reform, despite his consistent opposition to it in the past. Other Evangelical waverers were hauled into line by Carey's call to arms. The last-minute switch of these Evangelicals from the anti to the pro camp was the key factor in shifting the balance in the House of Laity.

In the chill dark air in Dean's Yard outside Church House, the announcement of the voting figures was followed by a profound hush as the crowd calculated the result. Then hundreds of candles were held aloft as supporters indulged in an unrestrained bout of cheering, weeping and hugging. A single firework burst like a flare in the night sky, fortifying the carnival atmosphere. A wave of emotion engulfed the gathering; for many, it was a liberation from a form of sexual apartheid. Above the crush, a banner was raised which reminded them that the 'struggle' went on. 'Congratulations sisters: Roman Catholic women next,' it read. Elaine Jones, one of the first women to be ordained a deacon in 1987, spoke for many when, in a no doubt unconscious echo of Geldard, she said: 'I felt I had been led on until I got to the point where there was a brick wall. God was calling me through that brick wall, but there was no way I could get through. General Synod has now done it for me and I can see now where God is calling me. It's just incredible.'

On steps at the rear of the building sat dazed, weeping opponents with their heads in their hands, each alone with his or her private grief. Others stumbled about like survivors of a train crash. Sickened by what they regarded as the triumphalist celebrations going on around them, they felt betrayed, hurt and abandoned. They also felt grievously misunderstood; their opposition to women priests, they felt, had not sprung from hatred of women or a love of power but from a deep-seated conviction that they must remain loyal to higher truths which, they fervently believed, God had revealed in the Scriptures. One announced to the television cameras his decision to resign his ministry 'with immediate effect'. Others considered their futures in silence. An Anglo–Catholic bishop sought solace in the chapel at Church House, where he wept alone for more than an hour. Almost unnoticed, the Synod was still in session inside Church House, and later that evening it overwhelmingly carried legislation to provide compensation to any full-time clergy who decided to leave the Church on conscientious grounds.

Carey was one of those quietly sharing the elation. One Synod member said of his speech: 'We got the impression that he might not have wanted to stay in office if the vote had gone the wrong way. Clearly his dream is to be the Archbishop who presides over the most fundamental change in the Church's ministry since St

Augustine. Now he has got his wish.' But Carey was also careful to be magnanimous in victory; like most of the bishops, he had agreed in advance that conciliation was a higher priority than celebration if the Church was to heal its self-inflicted wounds. He recalls seeking out David Hope, the Anglo-Catholic Bishop of London who was a leading opponent of women priests. 'I remember saying to David, who has been a very good friend of mine for many years, "David, we disagree over this matter but I want you to know how much I want to support you personally, and if there is any way I can help, come and see me." '

The official reactions were rolling off the photocopiers within minutes. Congratulatory messages arrived from all over the world. MOW predicted 'a fresh surge of energy, a raising of morale, a new credibility in the eyes of the world' for the Church. The Protestant Free Churches, including the Methodist Church, which had admitted women to the ministry 25 years earlier, expressed their delight. For them, the Church of England's belated decision to follow in their footsteps by appointing women as ministers was certain to prove beneficial. One of the central obstacles to closer links with the Church of England had been the fact that the Anglicans could not recognize their female ministers. Now that barrier had been torn down, the prospect of a new 'covenant' between the Free Churches and the Church of England was once again on the agenda. With the pendulum within the Church of England swinging from its catholic to its Protestant wing, such an alliance could bring the Free Churches firmly back into the mainstream.

Rome, predictably, sounded a jarring note. In a brief statement the Vatican's chief spokesman, the former bullfighter Dr Joaquin Navarro-Valls, said the Roman Catholic Church's stance on the issue – that the ordination of women priests would constitute a 'grave obstacle' to hopes of reunion between the Churches – had been emphasized by several Popes to successive Archbishops of Canterbury, most recently Carey. The Vatican was well aware that the Church of England's decision would provide a new impetus to the small but vociferous body of Roman Catholic feminists calling for similar equality in their Church, and the abruptness of its statement angered liberal English Roman Catholics. Cardinal Basil Hume, Archbishop of Westminister and head of Roman Catholics in England and Wales, was a little more emollient. The decision to ordain women was not simply a matter of equality or of justice, he said in a statement: 'Nor can it be decided exclusively because of the changed values and attitudes of society, significant though these are.' But the Cardinal also insisted that the Church of England's decision would not plunge ecumenical relations into a cold war – although the vote was to mark the beginning of a distinct chill. The search for reunion – the *raison d'être* of many on the Church of England's Anglo-Catholic wing – was once again on the back-burner. Immediately after the debate, Geldard had held out the prospect that disillusioned Anglo-Catholics (a thousand were thought to be in this category) might be able to negotiate special terms of entry into the Roman Catholic Church to ease what would inevitably be a traumatic transition. Although no formal talks had taken place, senior Roman Catholics were privately very sympathetic. They had been particularly dismayed at what they saw as the volte-face perpetrated in the debate by the Anglican Bishop of Birmingham, Mark Santer, who was the co-chairman of the long-running talks between the two Churches designed to heal the rift that had existed since the Reformation. In an influential speech, he played down the detrimental effect the ordination of women priests would have on relations with Rome, and declared himself in favour of the Measure. 'I used to believe that it was possible for us to wait for further consensus to develop; I have come to see that continued delay is in fact debilitating the life of the Church,' he said.

The vote evinced genuine shock in English Roman Catholic circles. In the following months, however, as leading Anglicans telegraphed their desire to convert, it was replaced with a barely disguised air of excitement. A vestigial hankering to 'reconvert' the country to Roman Catholicism surfaced briefly, fuelled unwittingly by Cardinal Hume himself. Indeed, a number of prominent Roman Catholics, calculating that the Synod's decision would further erode the Church of England's standing, scented an historic opportunity to promote the Roman Catholic Church as the natural heir to the mantle of 'national Church'. Their ambitions, however, owed more to the heady emotions of the moment, 'exuberant hubris' as one insider put it, than careful reflection. But there were signs of a slow shifting of the sands. While the prophecies of the demise of the Church of England were premature – as they had always been – there was a powerful sense that it had wrested itself loose from one of its moorings. On many occasions over the next few months, it would seem to have lost its centre of gravity.

Carey's immediate concern was to calm the turmoil within the Church of England, but his appeal for a period of quiet reflection and deep prayer – made at a packed news conference immediately after the vote – had, inevitably, come too late for some. Although the legislation was by no means clear of all its hurdles, most notably Parliament, they had already conceded defeat. For them, the essence of the Church of England had been irrevocably changed on 11 November. By even countenancing the ordination of women as priests, it had renounced its fundamental claim to be part (albeit separated) of the universal Church because it had radically altered its view of the nature of the priesthood. It had, as one put it, cut the umbilical cord. Almost overnight, they felt it seemed to have become an insignificant Protestant sect, rudderless and heading for the rocks. If this was an extreme view it articulated the feelings of those who believed something fundamental had taken place.

The day after the vote – the final day of the General Synod meeting – an atmosphere of confusion and panic pervaded Church House. The bishops, like most people, had been psychologically braced for the legislation to be defeated and were now in uncharted waters. Indeed, many of the middle-of-the-road bishops, though sympathetic to women priests, had privately hoped that the legislation would be defeated. 'I had thought in advance that the worst result would be for the legislation to squeeze through by a few votes,' said one Evangelical bishop who had voted in favour. 'Many of us felt that though some dioceses were ready for it others were not and another five years delay would help. It was almost a disappointing victory.' The traditionalist camp was, meanwhile, sending out conflicting signals. A handful of prominent figures had already indicated they were throwing in the towel, but traditionalist leaders were urging their constituency to wait. Anne Widdecombe, the Social Security minister whose brother was a clergyman in Bristol, had been one of the first to announce that she was leaving the Church after 27 years and was considering becoming a Roman Catholic. Many Anglo-Catholics had been taken by surprise by her statement; they had not realized she had been an ally. Widdecombe was received a few months later, somewhat ostentatiously, at the first sung Catholic mass to be held in the crypt of the Palace of Westminster since the Reformation. John Gummer, the then Agriculture Minister and a far more vociferous opponent of women priests, also indicated his intention to depart. At Church House, the shock which had stunned the traditionalists into silence the previous day had been replaced by bitterness and anger. A group of them pointedly boycotted the prayers in the Synod chamber; there were acrimonious scenes in corridors when they confronted liberal bishops. Many Anglo-Catholic Synod members had already gone home to lick their wounds. Such was the psychological trauma that many of them, almost unconsciously, slowly removed their black clerical shirts and dog collars and folded them away in a drawer, as if at the end of some formal occasion.

The nation had been transfixed by this bloodless civil war. The drama had all the ingredients of a soap opera penned by Anthony Trollope – sex, power and religion. Though fewer than five per cent of the population are regular Church of England churchgoers (still a higher percentage than attend football matches), many more feel affection for it as an institution inextricably entwined with English history. Its established status still gives it the duty to act as the conscience of the nation. The issue of women priests aroused deep emotions in people who had not darkened the door of a church since childhood except at weddings and funerals, perhaps because the debate exhumed unresolved tensions and prejudices about the role of women in society that were supposed to have been long buried. For some, the notion of women priests aroused deep antagonism, even a sense of indecency. Others were so consumed with outrage at the perceived injustice to women that they stopped their ears to any argument against female ordination. The issue briefly became a touchstone of 'political correctness', and public figures found themselves cross-examined about it on television opinion programmes.

Most people were, however, bemused by the ferocity with which normally mild-mannered churchmen and women engaged in battle. In the secular world, after all, the principle – if not always the practice – of equality between the sexes had been accepted some time ago, and enshrined in the Sex Discrimination Act. The Church's position seemed anachronistic. Surely it was a simple issue of justice that women should enjoy the same rights as men, so why were the dissenters threatening to split the Church over the issue? A woman had, until recently, been the unchallenged occupant of No 10 Downing Street, and had enjoyed a not inconsiderable influence over the appointing of Church of England bishops. Another woman, the Queen, was the Supreme Governor of the Church. Within the Church, however, the stakes were much higher. Beneath the surface ripples of scheming deans, overbearing Mrs Proudies and vacillating bishops, murkier currents were flowing.

As with the Conservative Party and European Union, the Anglican Church was split from top to bottom over the question of women priests. Like the Euro-sceptics, the antis were in the minority but were capable of inflicting heavy damage. Where the Euro-sceptics warned about the erosion of national sovereignty, the anti-women priest campaigners railed against the erosion of orthodoxy. As in Parliament, it was an issue that crossed party lines; Anglo-Catholics on one wing of the Church found themselves in an unlikely alliance with conservative Evangelicals on the other wing against the common enemy, the menace of liberalism. For them the ordination of women as priests was a Pandora's box; after the lid had been opened, out would pop women bishops, practising gay and lesbian clergy and feminist, pagan liturgies which referred to God as her. Some of them believed they were engaged in an almost Manichaean struggle for the very soul of the Church. To their sworn enemies, the traditionalists were rigid misogynists or repressed homosexuals whose only motive in wanting to retain an oppressive patriarchal system was to cling on to power. The pro-women camp had watched their counterparts in the secular world breaking down one barrier after another, bursting through what had come to be known as the 'glass ceiling'. Now the women in the Church wanted to smash through the 'stained glass ceiling'. Some felt that no price was too much to pay.

How had the Church reached this parlous position? Many Church members were little more than agnostic on the question of whether women should be priests. They were not convinced by the arguments either way. All they knew was that the Church was being torn apart and the issue had to be resolved. But one of the reasons that the Church had reached snapping point was that its decentralized structures for debate and decision had proved inadequate. At both national and international levels, the liberals – frustrated by the lumbering democratic process – had promoted their cause by breaking the rules. They often rushed ahead before the practical and theological implications had been thought through. The result was that the traditionalists felt profoundly threatened and their attitudes became entrenched. The initial impulse to ordain women as priests originated outside the Church of England, but once other provinces of the Anglican Communion – the worldwide Anglican Church – had unilaterally proceeded to ordain women, the pressure on the Church of England to fall into line became increasingly irresistible. The crisis which enveloped the Church of England can, in part, be traced to an event which occurred on the other side of the world fifty years ago.

2

Chinese Whispers

In the early months of 1944, a diminutive Chinese woman called Florence Tim Oi Li found herself working behind enemy lines in more senses than one. Not only had she been effectively stranded on a peninsula off southern China by the advance of the Japanese army, but she had also crossed into unknown theological territory. The latter action was to earn her the opprobrium of the Anglican establishment and, equally unsought, a place in its history.

Born Li Tim Oi in Hong Kong in May 1907, she was the daughter of a progressive doctor and teacher who had, in his youth, rejected Buddhism in favour of Christianity. He had, however, kept one foot in the old world by retaining the Chinese practice of keeping two women in his house, an official wife and a concubine – Li Tim Oi's mother. In her early 20s, Li Tim Oi enrolled in a colonial school and joined a local congregation in the Anglican diocese of Hong Kong, part of a province that covered much of southern China. Drawing many, but by no means all, of its leaders from the Church of England, it was a missionary Church operating in largely difficult and unpredictable conditions; as with early settlers in the American West, the first law was survival and normal rules had often to be suspended. English clergy working in China, unencumbered by the conventions of home, were also aware of the necessity – like the Jesuit missionaries before them – of evolving an indigenous form of Christianity in the region by adapting Anglicanism to the local culture. Thus, the branch of Anglicanism that Florence Tim Oi Li (she had by then Anglicized her name) chose to work for differed in subtle ways from the Church of England. The Christian name she had selected was her tribute to Florence Nightingale, though she was almost certainly unaware of the words reputedly written by the nurse in 1852: 'I would have given the Church my head, my hand, and my heart. She would not have them. She told me to go back and do crochet in my mother's drawing room.'

When the Japanese invaded Manchuria in 1937, intent on settling old squabbles with its neighbour, she was studying at a theological college in Canton, a target for aerial bombing. Ordained a deaconess in 1941 by the Bishop of Hong Kong, Ronald Hall (in contrast to the Church of England, there was no distinction between a deaconess and a deacon in the Chinese Anglican Church) she was posted to Macao, a Portuguese colony just 35 miles from Hong Kong which had become increasingly isolated by the Japanese advance. As a deaconess, she was authorized to baptize, marry and bury but not give absolution or celebrate Communion; those tasks were reserved for visiting priests. But as the Japanese grip tightened, travel to and from the Macao peninsula was restricted and, as a wartime exigency, she was given permission by a local bishop to celebrate Communion to ensure that her hungry and dispirited congregation, together with the refugees fleeing to the area, were not deprived of the sacraments. 'No one in Macao objected because I was female,' she later recalled, 'not even the British Consul.'

Tim Oi Li had not yet taken an irrevocable step, however. It was Hall who, on receiving reports of her activities, determined to recognize and 'regularize' her work by ordaining her as Anglicanism's first woman priest, an act, he was well aware, that was unprecedented and possibly illegal. Cut off from his fellow Chinese bishops by the war, Hall was effectively the senior bishop in the region. As an advocate of women priests, if no friend of strident feminism, the Oxford-educated Hall was more concerned with the theological anomaly of a lay person celebrating Communion (Tim Oi Li was technically still only a lay woman in the eyes of many) than female ordination. Later, he would justify his unilateral action by saying he was merely confirming what the Holy Spirit had already ordained. He was also pushing to its limits a principle which was to have

15

increasingly central a role in the women priest debate, that of provincial, or in this case diocesan, autonomy: the right of individual parts of the Church to strike out on their own.

Hall's efforts to inform others of his action, even in wartime, left something to be desired. In June 1943, he sent a letter informing the then Archbishop of Canterbury, Dr William Temple, of his intentions, explaining to his old friend that no 'prejudices' should deprive the congregations in his care of the sacraments. Then, the following January, unable to contact his fellow bishops and without waiting for the arrival of the Archbishop's reply, which had been delayed in the wartime postal system, he went ahead with the ordination. Temple, as Hall had no doubt expected, expressed grave disapproval, warning that the granting of temporary powers to Florence Tim Oi Li was one thing, but ordaining her would be an innovation far more difficult to reverse and as such should be resisted. When later told of the *fait accompli*, his response was also terse; he would withhold official comment until the Chinese bishops had reacted. Meanwhile, oblivious to the controversy, Florence Tim Oi Li, after a dangerous and arduous trek through Japanese-held territory to 'free' China, had been through her ordination ceremony in a small church in Zhaoqing. Before a small congregation of local Christians, Bishop Hall laid his hands on her head and recited: 'Take thou the authority to preach the Word of God, and to minister the holy Sacraments in the Congregation where thou shalt be lawfully appointed thereunto.'

In their conversations before the ceremony, the bishop appears to have been strangely reticent about discussing the unorthodox status to which she was to be elevated, and she seemed blithely unaware of the implications. 'We did not talk about my being the first woman to become a priest,' she recalled years later.

Or if he did, I don't remember, I took no notice of that. God had brought me through many dangers to that place, it strengthened my belief that it was his will that I become a priest. Here I was, a simple girl wishing to devote my life to his service. The wider issues of the ordination of women were far from my mind as I entered the little church. I was being obedient to God's call. The notion that this step I was taking would be controversial and have worldwide repercussions was something that never occurred to me until after I had returned to Macao and the war was over.

In early 1946, Tim Oi Li was summoned to the Bishop's office in Hong Kong to face a stark dilemma. Hall was away, but his secretary told her: 'The bishops at Lambeth Palace will not accept your ordination. Bishop Hall is in a very difficult situation. Either he resigns as a bishop, or you forfeit the title of priest.' Anxious to defuse a controversy which was far from all of her own making, she reverted to the traditional submissiveness of Chinese women, telling Bishop Hall in a letter that she was a 'mere worm' in relation to him, and that she did not need the title of priest if she could continue to serve God. But her submissive tone was not all it seemed; she assured friends that she never resigned her orders and that her letter was merely a means of allowing Hall to remain in office. In the broader context, however, what was important was that she had infiltrated male terrain.

When the news of what the *Church Times*, the Church of England's weightiest newspaper, was to describe dismissively as 'the incident' had filtered through to England two years earlier it had caused a ripple of surprise and anger. The traditionalist Anglo-Catholic wing protested and the *Church Times* thundered. Hall, it said, could have avoided raising questions of sacramental validity or loyalty to Church order. Instead, he had 'preferred to play a lone hand, not like a civilized leader who is himself subject to constitutional authority but like a wild man of the woods.' The newspaper laid down the prevailing traditionalist line:

In Christ there is neither male nor female. This is undoubtedly true of personal capacity for spiritual attainment. Nevertheless, even in Christ the sexes remain physically distinct, and there is nothing in the Bible to show they are not designedly differentiated as completely in ministerial function in the Church which Christ founded, as they are in the natural world which God created. It is a matter of decisive

17

significance for all present practical purposes that Christ admitted to the apostolate neither the women who ministered to Him nor the mother who bore Him.

This view did not go unchallenged, however. The *Methodist Recorder* attacked the intemperate tone of the editorial, referring to a growing movement in favour of the ordination of women priests. In the letters' page of the *Church Times*, amid its coverage of the war, the small ads and items with headings such as 'A gold spittoon for Queen Victoria', the debate spluttered for weeks. One correspondent recalled with relish a priest who had told a woman: 'Madam, you are no more capable of being ordained a priest than I am of having a baby.' But the newspaper also noted that, in Hall's former parish of St Luke's, Newcastle, the parishioners backed him 'one hundred per cent' and 'his affirmation that the Christian should not care two hoots about what anybody thinks is being quoted with approval.' At the end of 1944, however, the Church of England's Council for the Defence of Church Principles - an influential Anglo-Catholic organization - issued a strongly worded statement which almost certainly sealed Tim Oi Li's fate. It warned: 'If the woman in question is allowed to continue to minister as a priest, there will be a major crisis throughout the Anglican Communion.'

Archbishop Temple, a socially progressive Anglo-Catholic who was opposed to women priests on practical as much as theological grounds, was torn between maintaining the *status quo* and showing flexibility towards the needs of the missionary branches of the Church. Nevertheless, he was concerned about the breach of discipline. In an official letter, he deplored the ordination and accused Hall of acting *ultra vires*. 'I cannot think that in any circumstances whatever an individual bishop has the right to take such a step which is most certainly contrary to all the laws and precedents of the Church,' he wrote. Although the letter was never signed by Temple because he died in October 1944 before it could be sent, his sentiments were endorsed by his successor, Dr Geoffrey Fisher, who relayed them to Hall in no uncertain terms during a tense interview at Lambeth Palace the following year. But Fisher had no legal jurisdiction over the Chinese Church - the individual provinces of the worldwide Anglican Church were technically independent of each other though bound by ties of loyalty – and Hall maintained his intransigence, refusing even to suspend Tim Oi Li pending a ruling by his colleagues, the Chinese bishops. When Fisher's opinion was later sought by the Chinese bishops, he advised them to repudiate Hall's action and forbid Tim Oi Li to continue as a priest. 'It grieves me greatly to advise you to take this course,' wrote Fisher, a former public school headmaster.

> Bishop Hall is so good and glorious that to rebuke him in this way is beyond words grievous. He did a thing which was *ultra vires* with every good motive. He has refused the advice of friends to suspend the woman and to await the judgement of the Church. He has not allowed himself to be helped but has simply said obstinately, I know I am right. Grievous though it may be, it seems to me to be the duty of your House to say to him, You are wrong.

At their meeting in Shanghai in March 1946, the Chinese House of Bishops decided that Tim Oi Li should resign from the priesthood and they rapped Hall across the knuckles. Hall reluctantly accepted Tim Oi Li's resignation, but at the Chinese Church's General Synod in 1947, he once again sought to force the issue of women priests on to the agenda by proposing an experimental period of 20 years in which deaconesses might be ordained to the priesthood. The Synod warily sidestepped what was a very radical proposal, deciding instead to ask the Lambeth Conference, the worldwide Anglican Church's ten-yearly council of bishops which next met in 1948, whether such an experiment would be in accordance with Anglican tradition and order.

The 'incident' in China had rekindled in England a debate about women priests which had been dormant since the early years of the century. But the potential for such a divisive internal conflict had always existed. Since the Church of England was established by the Elizabethan Settlement in the sixteenth century, it has always held in an uneasy tension two theoretically mutually exclusive extremes. On the one hand there are the Protestant reformers or Evangelicals –

whose formularies of faith such as the Thirty-nine Articles specifically bar flirtations with 'Popish' practices; on the other are the Catholics, who saw the Anglican Church as temporarily separated but never divorced from the Roman Catholic and Orthodox traditions. These two groups formed their own subcultures and tribal loyalties and throughout the history of the Church, one or other has usually been dominant. The Catholics experienced one of their high points in the last century with the revival of the Anglo-Catholic movement by John Henry (later Cardinal) Newman. This movement emphasized the importance of ritual, vestments and the continuity of tradition guaranteed by an unbroken chain of orthodox bishops that could be traced back to the apostles. Indeed, Newman famously converted to the Roman Catholic Church partly because of his doubts about whether the Church of England could justifiably claim to have upheld this apostolic succession. Members of the movement therefore have a very strong idea of Church structure, order and discipline. The movement's adherents are rarely seen out of clerical uniform and like to be addressed as Father; they follow many Roman Catholic practices, 'smells and bells' in church and devotion to the Virgin Mary. The more antiquarian and camp of them (there has always been a strong if often latent homosexual streak running through the movement) don birettas, the flamboyant caps worn by Roman Catholic monsignori. Crucially, however, most of them share the Roman Catholic 'high' view of the priesthood, that the symbolic role of the priest in representing Christ at the Last Supper is more than just a piece of play acting. At the celebration of Communion, the consecration of the bread and wine, the priest represents the 'very person' of Christ. Because Christ was male, maleness and the priestly ministry are inextricably entwined. To ensure that the sacrament is efficacious (that the bread and wine somehow 'become' the body and blood of Christ), the person presiding must be an ordained male.

The Evangelicals, whose luminaries include social reformers such as Wilberforce and Shaftesbury, are a different breed. Instead of tradition they put their emphasis on Scripture, and they are suspicious of anything they believe has no biblical basis (such as the Roman Catholic practice of devotion to Mary). They have less regard for Church order because they believe that local churches should be power bases, and they tend towards a 'low' Protestant view of the priesthood – the priest as representative of the community of believers. For some of them, the priest – or minister – is little more than a trained lay person appointed as a leader in the community; the idea of an apostolic succession is alien. Evangelicals tend to eschew clerical dress in favour of suits and ties and prefer the informality of Christian names; the 'happy clappy' element prefers tambourines and guitars to Byrd and Palestrina, and on the fringes lurk the charismatics and those who 'speak in tongues' or 'faint in the spirit'. For Evangelicals, the main focus of church services is the sacrament of the Word, the readings and preaching. Many of them do not believe that anything supernatural occurs at Communion, and see it instead as a special reminder of the Last Supper. Some would argue that, because the concept of ordination never occurs in Scriptures, an unordained, lay person has just as much right as a priest to preside at Communion.

These two wings – the 'high and hazy' and the 'low and crazy' – have an immense influence, but the great bulk of the Church of England, its ballast, is made up of those in the middle, the so-called Broad Church. An amalgam of the Catholic and Evangelical strands, they display a benign tolerance to the enthusiasms and eccentricities of those on the extremes. In recent years, however, a new force has energized them – liberalism. Anglicanism has never had a single coherent authoritative body of theology to which to appeal; it has survived through a series of pragmatic compromises. Checks and balances between the various parties have evolved through history, particularly in the various forms of democratic government set up to ensure that every group can feel represented. The overall impression is one of homogeneity, but appearances can be deceptive. Outwardly, the Anglican Church, with its hierarchy of bishops, priests and deacons, mirrors the structures of the Roman Catholic Church. Inwardly, however, its Protestant character reasserts itself and it instinctively recoils from any discipline imposed from above. One traditionalist summed up the effect of the November 1992 vote thus:

Anglicanism is really three strange bedfellows in a very bumpy bed. What happened was that each of the three parties could only exist by denying the other two. I could, as an Anglo-Catholic, say to myself that I represented the real mind of the Church of England, and simultaneously, the Evangelical could say to himself that he represented the real mind of the Church of England. We would each unChurch each other by saying we were the real Church of England. I could do that until November and, by wonderful mental gymnastics and semantics, believe it. One thing we were all able to do this over was the ordained ministry. I think that what has happened is that the scales have fallen from people's eyes.

It was the suffragettes of the nineteenth century rather than the liberals of the twentieth who gave the feminist movement its first impetus. It was largely in response to their pressure for the Church to recognize the role of women such as Florence Nightingale that the somewhat artificial order of deaconesses was created in the 1860s. The development was, ironically, welcomed by the Anglo-Catholics, who saw it as a perfectly valid revival of an early Church practice which had fallen into abeyance in the medieval period. They did not regard the order as one of the holy orders – the traditional triumvirate of bishop, priests and deacon established by the early Church. Deaconesses were, therefore, technically only particularly committed lay women with a clerical-sounding title. But this distinction was never clearly spelt out, and there was always some ambiguity over their status; the more militant of them insisted they had been properly ordained and their order was one of the 'holy' orders. They were to exploit this area of ambiguity to press their case for the ordination of women as priests. The notion of women in the priesthood was still unthinkable by the vast majority. But the assumption that a modern generation had no right or authority to change nearly 2,000 years of Church custom and practice fixed by the early Church Fathers was, by then, no longer universal. As scholars began to challenge a literal interpretation of the Bible, women were able to question those sections of Scripture upon which the traditionalists built their case that women should be subordinate to men, including the Genesis story that Eve was created from Adam's rib. From very early on, the debate attracted interest far beyond the confines of the pew and the cloister; it provided a visual manifestation of profound shifts of attitude which were stirring in society at large.

The belief that men and women should fulfil distinct, if complementary, roles in the 'created order' has underpinned many of the arguments used by the opponents of the ordination of women priests. As the *Church Times* put it in the 1940s, the differentiation between the sexes has been held to be a fundamental fact of creation; unlike a person's race or colour, a person's gender is, in this view, a defining characteristic. To blur this divinely-ordained distinction – which is spiritual and psychological as well as biological – is to obscure, even deny, God's 'blueprint' for humanity and invite spiritual chaos. Though male and female attributes are mixed in every personality (the argument goes), masculine and feminine traits can be broadly identified: men tend to be the aggressors and take the initiative; women tend to be creative and receptive. To illustrate this thesis, one Anglo-Catholic bishop often used to form an 'O' with the thumb and index finger of his left hand and slide the index finger of his right hand through it in a crude sexual gesture recognizable around the world. 'It's as simple as that,' he would explain to his audience, bemused by the incongruity of a bishop making such a sign. 'I use the analogy of electricity,' he would continue solemnly. 'The man is the plug and the woman is the socket. It is the same throughout nature. You can't buck creation.' The argument would have struck a chord with his predecessors, even if the gesture might not. The qualities of women, though admirable, were therefore not appropriate to the priesthood; a woman priest could never, by her nature, fully express the essence of masculinity and therefore her representation of the male Christ could never be complete. For many Evangelicals, this view was supported by Scripture, which appeared to bar women from leadership roles in the Church. The natural and dignified role of the woman, the traditionalists argued, was best exemplified in the conduct of Christ's demure mother Mary. Though few could have been better aware of her son's wishes, she was never reported to have preached or performed any priestly functions.

The volunteer army of women who kept the church pews polished and made the jam for the parish fete were largely satisfied with this view of their role. But as early as the late 1800s, a group of them had made some headway in increasing their voice in the Church's democratic councils. Doughty suffragettes like the Cheltenham Ladies' College-educated Maude Royden, who challenged the Church leadership in the early years of this century, also added momentum. Royden defied the then Bishop of London after he had banned women from preaching during a wartime evangelical campaign. To the fury of the Evangelicals, who suspected a feminist plot, she took up invitations from progressive Anglican churches to proclaim her views from the pulpit. In 1919, she was to have delivered the Good Friday sermon at St Botolph's, Bishopsgate, in the City of London, but when parishioners arrived they found a note pinned to the door saying she had been banned. Undaunted, Royden preached in the adjoining parish hall. Many found her action shocking, and a petition deploring her behaviour garnered 1,000 signatures. Two years later, after a similar incident, the London clergy decided by 195 votes to 111 that it was 'generally inexpedient and contrary to the interests of the Church that women should publicly minister in consecrated buildings.' The vote did little, however, to deter Royden and others from using the pulpit as a political soapbox. Women significantly enhanced their rights to be represented in the Church's democratic councils after their secular counterparts won women the right (if they were 30 or over and householders or married to householders) to vote in Parliamentary general elections. When parochial church councils were first established in the 1890s to involve the laity in the management of parishes, women had been excluded. They also had no right to sit on the Representative Church Council, an early version of the General Synod. In 1919, out of embarrassment at the anomaly as much as anything else, women were granted the right to be elected to parochial church councils and the Representative Church Council.

But the bar on women climbing further up the ministerial ladder, or even clambering onto the bottom rung, was confirmed by the Lambeth Conference of 1920 – the sixth in the series of ten-yearly gatherings of Anglican bishops from the branches of the worldwide Church. Though not binding, conference resolutions carried, and still carry, great moral weight as significant expressions of the opinions of the Anglican episcopate. In those years, unsurprisingly, it was still dominated by the Church of England, the 'mother Church'. It was this conference that really muddied the waters over the status of deaconesses. Although a preparatory committee set up to examine the ministry of women concluded that the order of deaconesses was a holy order, the conference's final statement failed to spell this out. The conference did, however, recommend that an 'authentic' form of ordination be used, and it went some way to define the role of the deaconess; she could, it decreed, 'lead in prayer' and, with the permission of her bishop, 'instruct and exhort the congregation'. Significantly absent from her responsibilities, however, were those functions still reserved for male deacons, such as assisting with the chalice at Communion and reading the Gospel. At least one of the bishops at Lambeth is thought to have put his foot down, arguing that deaconesses would only be allowed inside the altar rails over his dead body

Many deaconesses ordained in the 1920s nevertheless believed they had been admitted to holy orders, so the next Lambeth Conference, in 1930, came as a severe blow. It added nothing to the list of duties the deaconess could perform, but its preparatory committee on the issue specifically stated that deaconesses were 'outside the historic order of the ministry'. Not until the 1968 Lambeth Conference was it recommended that the order of deaconess be declared one of the 'holy orders'. Within the Church of England, however, this step was never made, though the deaconesses' role was extended in the 1970s. The issue was overtaken in the 1980s, however, when women were allowed to become deacons. Other branches of Anglicanism, which were not legally bound by the Church of England's decisions, took a more flexible view. It was this growing disparity of practice between the constituent Churches of the Anglican Communion which was to create increasing friction within it as years passed.

The intervention of the Second World War, and the waning of the feminist movement in general, resulted in a respite from the battle of the sexes, albeit a temporary one. The discussion of the issue by the 1948 Lambeth Conference (its start had been delayed by the war) had been forced upon it by the actions of the diocese of Hong Kong, which seemed remote to many both geographically and in understanding. The Church of England, with its customary insularity, still believed itself impervious to the pressures brought to bear by its still youthful, if increasingly unruly, progeny. Like the anti-colonialism which grew with the decline of the British Empire, a similar desire for independence grew in the outposts of Anglicanism. As the missionary churches developed, they nevertheless retained a family loyalty to the Church of England and the Archbishop of Canterbury. The Anglican Communion, the ecclesiastical version of the Commonwealth, evolved to preserve these ties; the Lambeth Conferences - presided over by the Archbishop of Canterbury at, until recently, Lambeth Palace, his grandiose but notoriously uncomfortable residence on the Thames overlooking the Houses of Parliament - provided a forum for friendship and debate. Significantly, however, the conferences had been born out of a need to settle theological disputes, but the original idea of a council authorized to define doctrine was quickly abandoned because of strenuous opposition. From a very early stage the principle of the autonomy of the individual Churches, within vaguely defined parameters, was set. As one early conference put it, the individual Anglican Churches or provinces around the world, which each had their own General Synods or the equivalent, 'are bound together, not by a central legislative and executive authority, but by a mutual loyalty sustained through the common counsel of the bishops in conference.' This lack of central authority - a deliberate contrast to the power structures of the Roman Catholic Church - was to prove as much a weakness as a strength as the women priests debate gathered momentum.

But when the issue of the ordination of Florence Tim Oi Li came before the 1948 conference, Fisher's hard line reflected the majority view. The conference's response to the query from the diocese of Hong Kong about whether deaconesses might be ordained to the priesthood for a twenty-year experimental period was an emphatic 'no'. Such an experiment, it decreed, would be 'against the tradition and the order and would gravely affect the internal affairs of the Anglican Communion'. Tim Oi Li heard of the conference decision while in the United States. She was the only female member of a delegation of Chinese clergy, and was under strict instructions to maintain a low profile and not to disclose that she was the Chinese woman who had caused such a furore by being ordained a priest and then being forced to renounce her orders. But word of her presence leaked out, and she was forced to abandon a planned trip to England to visit her sister who lived in Liverpool. After a few months she returned to China, and spent much of the rest of her life behind the bamboo curtain erected by Mao Tse-tung. Her life was made particularly miserable during the Cultural Revolution because she was both a Christian and someone 'tainted' by her contact with 'Western imperialism'. She was unable to leave again for more than thirty years, by which time Hong Kong had carried out the first official ordinations of two women priests and the issue was once more straining the fragile unity of the Church.

3

The Sixties

The 1960s were, first and foremost, the decade of sex. Like a dam burst, they unleashed the pill, the Lady Chatterley obscenity trial, sexual equality, homosexual rights and 'free' love. Drugs and radical politics added to the heady cocktail; at times, the mainstream Christian churches, regarded by the young as the custodians of Victorian prudery, seemed impotent against the tide. But to the traditionalists within the Church, it was also the era of an even more insidious influence – relativism, the philosophy that metaphysical and moral truths had no objective basis but were matters of subjective judgement. This had a knock-on effect on theology, and the new liberal thinking permeated many of the Anglican theological colleges which, at the time, were training the church leaders of the next generation. As one Anglo-Catholic bishop puts it:

> The most significant changes that took place since the war were the philosophical ones. Ontology was discounted and functionalism took its place. Traditional Christian belief does depend very considerably on ontology, what we are by creation, what we are by grace. I would maintain that ontology was written right into the heart of the biblical gospel and once you get away from what you are as a person or as a Church, then you take the view that things are determined by what you do and there is really no holding back.

Many Anglican churchmen found themselves increasingly swept

along by the prevailing liberal currents, epitomized in the public mind by the high-pitched Bishop of Woolwich, John Robinson, who outraged conservative opinion with his work of popular theology *Honest to God*, a naive attempt to demythologize traditional Christianity. Dr Michael Ramsey, the Archbishop of Canterbury, even appeared on television with Mick Jagger. In the early part of the decade, the issue of women priests seemed barely on the official agenda; it remained largely a genteel pamphlet war fought by academic theologians, far removed from the real action. But out of the public eye, informal networks of like-minded women were forming, bound by a common feeling of frustration.

Almost in parallel, however, the timetable for another project was being drawn up, the goal of which was hardly compatible with female ordination. The decision of Pope John XXIII to convene the Second Vatican Council in Rome before his death in 1963 made the prospect of reunion with Anglicanism plausible. For some time before Vatican II, cooperation had been growing between a number of Roman Catholic leaders and their Protestant counterparts. In 1961, Vatican-accredited observers were guests for the first time at the World Council of Churches, the idealistic, but increasingly politicized, ecclesiastical version of the United Nations. The changed atmosphere was reflected by Geoffrey Fisher's cordial, if unofficial, visit to John XXIII in 1960. Vatican II pumped helium into the unity balloon. In a series of sessions staged between 1962 and 1965, it not only decentralized power within the Catholic Church by devolving more authority to the bishops in individual countries, but it laid greater stress on the role of the laity and of the Church as a community of people as well as a hierarchical institution, bringing it closer to the Anglican model. Most importantly, it re-emphasized the biblical imperative of Christian unity. All this was exhilarating to those in the Anglican Church who – conscious that division undermined the essential message of the gospels – dreamed of a reunited Christendom. At last, Roman Catholicism seemed to Anglicans to be shedding some of the dubious accretions of the Counter-Reformation; the elusive grail of reunion was within reach.

One radical student leader was so fired by the prospect of the reconciliation of the Western Christian traditions that he forsook left-wing politics and revolutionary rhetoric for the Anglican priest-hood. In the 1960s, Peter Geldard, president of the student union at King's College, London, was a familiar figure at the anti-Vietnam rallies, student sit-ins and peace marches. During the 1968 riots in Paris, he was one of the delegates dispatched to the Sorbonne by the National Union of Students to demonstrate youthful solidarity. 'I was very left wing in those days,' he now recalls. 'The student world was given the impression, rightly or wrongly, that it was changing the world.' By 1971, when he was ordained by the then Archbishop of Canterbury, Michael Ramsey, he had a new crusade: unity with Roman Catholicism and the Orthodox Churches. Geldard, who had married a teacher, had come to believe that society should be reformed through a spiritual rather than a materialistic process. Hardly the stereotypical reactionary misogynist, though something of a purist, he was to become as committed an opponent of women priests as he had once been a proponent of radical political causes.

A different kind of radicalism was surfacing on the other side of the Atlantic. With the publication in the 1950s of the existentialist Simone de Beauvoir's *The Second Sex*, the feminist's 'bible', the women's movement was given a new impetus which was to permeate every facet of society. The appearance in 1963 of Betty Friedan's best-seller *The Feminine Mystique* – which argued that both sexes have the same innate abilities but society had suppressed those of women – marked the start of the second wave. Unlike the original women's movement which had aimed to achieve equal rights on the same terms as men, the new wave also began to demand the radical restructuring of society, even, in its most extreme forms, the eradica-tion of the male sex. Man's privileged social position, rather than capitalism, was seen as the cause of all oppression. Some feminists wanted to do away with women's 'enslaving' child-bearing role, rele-gating the task of the production of children to scientists in laborato-ries (something which seemed like science fiction then but is increasingly possible today). Crucially, their arguments promoted the 'functionalist' idea of the essential androgyny of the sexes, that the only real difference between male and female were a few biolog-ical appendages (which could, after all, be altered by surgery). This began to erode the traditionalists' position that the differences

30

between the sexes was profound and God-given, an 'ontological' fact of creation.

Much of this new thinking was taken on board by Church feminists in the United States. Influential American writers such as Rosemary Radford Ruether and Mary Daly, a former Roman Catholic nun who coined the phrase 'if God is male, then the male is God', saw their mission as toppling the Church's masculine image of God. Pressure began to mount not only for equal status between men and women within the Church but also for a wholesale rewriting of the sacred texts in language which expunged male imagery. As Daly put it in an essay entitled 'Why speak about God?':

> As the essential victims of the archaic God projections, women can bring this process of creativity into a new phase. This involves iconoclasm, the breaking of idols. The basic idol breaking will be done on the level of male superiority, on the plane of exorcizing them from consciousness and from the cultural institutions that breed them.

Ruether has invoked the powerful goddesses of paganism, such as Isis, to bolster her assault on the 'patriarchal' God. One of the most striking symbols used by the radical feminists depicted a near naked woman, a crown of thorns around her head, nailed to a cross. The feminists argued that men had traditionally either put women on a pedestal, like the Virgin Mary, or treated them as temptresses like Eve. Both approaches denied women's true personality. They blamed the resistance to women priests on male taboos such as an irrational terror of female menstruation (women had been barred from the inner courts of Jewish temples because they were regarded as 'unclean'). They were also to exploit the Achilles heel of the Anglo-Catholic movement, the prevalence of repressed homosexuality in its ranks. But Anglo-Catholics denied this strand of their character made any difference to their views. Many homosexual clergy were in favour of women priests – indeed the militant homosexual lobby often tried to link the two issues – and the feminists themselves included lesbians within their ranks.

While the Church feminist movement failed to sway the vast mass of churchgoers, it had an undeniable impact on progressive Church leaders. By challenging the validity of the traditional vision of God as essentially masculine, the movement reopened the question of why the priesthood remained closed to women. Aligned as it often was with the black civil rights movement, it was particularly influential within the American Episcopal Church – the United States branch of Anglicanism. In 1965, for example, the Bishop of California (where else?) proposed to ordain a deaconess as a deacon in order to 'put beyond doubt' her status in holy orders. After immediate protests, and a warning from the Vatican about the effect of such an innovation on relations between the Churches, the bishop referred the proposal to his colleagues in the House of Bishops, who declared that a deaconess could not administer Communion. It was, however, a sign of things to come.

Although real pressure for women priests did not begin to bubble up in the Church of England until the later part of the decade, the issue was never far from the surface, a fact inadequately appreciated by many of the Anglo-Catholics. The Congregationalists, a low-church denomination, had admitted women ministers since 1918. The English Presbyterian Church accepted the principle in 1921, ordaining its first woman minister in the 1950s. Ignoring John Knox's famous rant against the monstrous regiment of women, the Church of Scotland ordained women in 1969 in the face of relatively minor opposition. The Methodist Church, which of all the Churches had the greatest affinity with Anglicanism – its founder, John Wesley, remained an Anglican clergyman to the end of his days – had passed a series of resolutions in its Conferences since the 1930s approving the principle of women ministers. The secular landscape was changing even faster: women were being appointed to positions in the academic world, the law and politics that would have been unimaginable 50 years before. In 1962, partly in response to pressure from the World Council of Churches, which had waged a vigorous campaign for sexual equality since its inception, and partly as the result of another Church of England report, *Gender and Ministry*, the Archbishops of Canterbury and York (Michael Ramsey and Donald Coggan) established a top-level commission to examine the controversy. Under the chairmanship of the Bishop of Chester,

Gerald Ellison, an impressive line-up of theologians, experts and representatives of both sides of the debate (although critics pointed out that their average age was 57) laboured for four years to produce an inconclusive report, *Women and Holy Orders,* the verdict of which was that the development would be divisive.

Ramsey's appointment to Canterbury in 1961 almost certainly marked the zenith of the influence of Anglo-Catholicism this century. Combining the craggy Old Testament visage of an Eastern patriarch with the other-worldliness of an old-style Cambridge don (which he had been), his initial reaction when change was first mooted was usually negative. Over time, however, he would modify his attitude. He began his period in office opposed to women priests, but ended it apparently resigned to the development. While Archbishop of York, he answered a query about his stance on women priests by stating the classic Anglo-Catholic position: that while the Christian Church had enhanced the status of women, Christ had chosen only male apostles, and the question had to be looked at in relation to the whole issue of Christian unity. He added, however: 'I am very ready to have a good look at the possibility of change, knowing that God does reveal new truth to us after lapses of time.' In his early years at Canterbury, he remained convinced, however, that only a worldwide council of all the Christian Churches, including the Roman Catholic and Orthodox, had the authority to bless such a momentous break with the tradition of the centuries. In 1964, when he was asked by a female student when there would be women priests, he replied, his bushy eyebrows bobbing up and down in emphasis: 'Millions and millions and millions of years.'

It was he who initiated the first formal unity talks between Anglicans and Roman Catholics since the Reformation when he travelled to Rome to meet Pope Paul VI in 1966, an encounter he found profoundly moving. When he arrived in Rome – dodging Ian Paisley's ultra-Protestant, black armband-wearing protesters at the airport – he found a Pope with whom he could do business. At a private meeting in the Pope's library in the Vatican, Paul VI promised to review the Catholic refusal, dating from 1896, to recognize Anglican holy orders as valid, and to set up a joint commission of theologians to try to bridge the divide between the two Churches.

Near the end of the visit, Ramsey was taken aback when the Pope publicly removed from his finger the gold and diamond-encrusted ring he had been given by the city of Milan when Archbishop there and put it in Ramsey's palm. It was an eloquent gesture.

By the time of the 1968 Lambeth Conference, however, Ramsey recognized that a major shift of opinion was underway in the more progressive parts of the worldwide Anglican Church in favour of ordaining women . Ultimately, he had no more than moral authority to prevent other provinces doing more or less as they pleased within the confines of their own constitutions; as 'first among equals', all he could do was appeal to their loyalty. This lack of power seemed of minor importance at the time, because few foresaw that the issue of women priests and bishops could do serious damage to the Anglican Church. Like many others involved in the unity process, Ramsey convinced himself that Rome might anyway be moving towards opening the Roman Catholic priesthood to women, a view encouraged by many liberal Roman Catholic theologians. Similar sentiments also surfaced in other parts of the world, and there were no doubt those Roman Catholics who encouraged unilateral action by the Anglicans in the belief that it would have a knock-on effect on their own Church. But the Anglican hope that Rome was on the brink of reversing centuries of tradition had more basis in wishful thinking than reality, and reflected a misunderstanding of the workings of the Vatican, which (until relatively recently anyway) allowed its theologians to follow the winds of speculation while keeping a firm hand on the orthodox tiller. While women had undoubtedly been accorded a higher status within Catholic ranks since Vatican II, ordaining them was never on the agenda; such reforms took centuries, not decades. The Vatican was, however, culpable to the extent that it had failed to give the Anglicans the appropriate warning signals. The cautions of Anglo-Catholics about the disastrous impact that the ordination of women priests would have on the prospects for unity with the Roman Catholics could therefore be too easily brushed aside. In the 1966 *Women and Holy Orders* report, the contributor on the Church of England's relations with the 'Roman' Church felt able to say that: 'As an impediment to reunion, the matter was not apparently of great significance.'

The findings of Ramsey's 1966 commission seems to have made little impact on his personal thinking about female ordination. Its 190-page report pleased few: while proponents of female ordination decried its lack of recommendations for action, their critics derided its lack of theological analysis. Proponents of women priests, it said, were convinced that a new insight had been awoken by the 'spirit of the times' in which the 'now discredited biological and theological assumptions' about women would be discarded; scriptural injunctions that men and women had been created equal in the sight of God should be incarnated in a female priesthood. Those opposed, the report continued, felt there was no justification in Scripture, that it was contrary to tradition and disruptive to relations with other Churches, that there was a profound psychological difference between men and women and that maleness was crucial to the symbolism of the priest.

Opponents of women priests have tended to fall into two categories, the Anglo-Catholics and the conservative Evangelicals. For the Anglo-Catholics, any authority that the Anglican Church could be said to possess was derived from the fact that it was a part of the universal Church – the 'one holy, catholic and apostolic Church' as the creed puts it – which could trace its history back to the apostles. The Anglican Church's priestly orders gained validity because they were a continuation of the historic orders found in the universal Catholic Church, the main branches of which were Roman Catholicism and Orthodoxy. At ordination, the bishops who lay hands on the head of the priest are part of an unbroken chain reaching back to St Peter, from whom the Roman Catholic Pope takes his authority. The fact that the universal Church had never ordained women to the priesthood (even in the early Church when the guiding influence of the Holy Spirit was arguably at its strongest) weighed heavily with them, as did the fact that both the Roman Catholic and Orthodox Churches – which made up the vast mass of the universal Church – were still against doing so. They did not believe that the Anglican Church alone had the authority to overturn this unbroken tradition of 2,000 years of a male priesthood; any such decision could justifiably be made only in concert with their partners, particularly if they were genuine in their claims to want reunion. If they made a unilateral decision to ordain women, they were effectively cutting themselves adrift.

For the majority of Anglo-Catholics, the issue of women priests also went to the heart of their beliefs about faith and order. Although the New Testament says nothing directly about women priests, something of Christ's intentions for his Church can, they argue, be divined from his actions. First, he chose to become incarnate as a man. Second, he chose only male apostles. Although he was mould-breaking in many respects, including in his treatment of women in general, he deliberately never elevated a woman to the status of an apostle. The Anglo-Catholics are dismissive of those who argue that Christ was a victim of cultural conditioning and that, if he returned today, he would have appointed female apostles. How, they ask, can the Son of God be said to be constrained by anything? He was revolutionary in other areas – he challenged the established religious and secular assumptions of the time – so why not this one? If he intended that women should fulfil priestly functions, why did he choose to become a man in a male-dominated society, and then select only male apostles? To the Anglo-Catholics, Christ's actions are totally consistent with their understanding of the pattern of creation in which the male is the initiator and the female the receptor. The theme is repeated again and again in biblical imagery; particularly powerful is the symbol of the Church as the bride of Christ. If the priest is required to represent the very person of Christ at Communion, therefore, a woman cannot adequately fulfil this role, either as a visual symbol (sexual symbols are deeply ingrained in the psyche) or inwardly. Few Anglo-Catholics would say that it would be impossible for a woman to be a priest; most would say that, on this understanding of the priesthood, there is a very large element of doubt that a woman can be ordained. If a woman priest celebrates Communion, therefore, no one can be absolutely certain that the bread and wine can actually represent the body and blood of Christ. To meddle with something so mysterious as the priesthood – especially if one, small part of the universal Church is going out on a limb – is to court disaster. If the sacraments are put in doubt, everything else is.

The conservative Evangelicals' position is simpler, though just as contentious; it relies on several key passages of St Paul, the apostle whose letters to various parts of the early Church form the basis of much current Church practice. St Paul appears quite clear on the subject – in the tradition of the Genesis story, women are subordinate to men. The head of every man is Christ and the husband is the head of his wife, he wrote (1 Corinthians 11.3). The man is the image and glory of God and woman is the glory of man (1 Corinthians 11.7). More controversially, St Paul wrote that women were to keep silent in church and that they should learn in silence and subjection and not teach (1 Corinthians 14.34; 1 Timothy 2.12). To the conservative Evangelical, therefore, only men can take the leadership role of teaching and expounding the Scriptures that is usually identified with priesthood. In fact, with the advent of team ministries, in which a team of clergy is led by a senior clergyman, many conservative Evangelicals modified their stance; they see no problem with a woman priest as such (female ordination is nowhere outlawed in Scripture and they do not believe that anything supernatural happens at Communion anyway). But a woman priest could never lead a team ministry, only be a member of it.

The argument in favour of ordaining women (which has won over many mainstream Evangelicals and Catholics who were adamantly opposed to the rest of the liberal agenda) is underpinned by another key Pauline phrase, that, in baptism, 'there is no such thing as Jew and Greek, slave and free man, male or female; for you are all one person in Jesus Christ' (Galatians 3.28). Unlike St Paul's other misogynistic, culturally-conditioned remarks, this phrase seems far more resonant to many Anglicans, particularly seen in the wider context of Christ's desire to embrace people who were on the margins of society of the time. The Church, the liberals argue, is constantly changing, and tradition can justifiably be modified if it remains consonant with the central truths of the faith. The Church has, after all, declared itself against slavery although a literal reading of some biblical passages would appear to support it. The ordination of women as priests is in accord with the spirit, if not always the letter, of the Scriptural tenets of faith because it fulfils St Paul's vision of a Church in which the artificial distinctions between men and women had been removed. The need to remove these distinctions in the Church has been prompted by changes in society at large; whereas the tradition of a male-only priesthood may have been valid in the context of past societies, the Holy Spirit has provided a new generation with a new way of looking at old truths. God is neither male nor female, and the important fact about Christ's incarnation was not that he came as a man but that he came as a human, to save all. If the role of the priest is to represent the community, the ordained person must reflect all important aspects of that community. A priest ordained by a bishop in that context is not, therefore, breaking with apostolic tradition or endangering the validity of Communion. Ordaining women is not merely a response to pressure to conform with fashionable, secular notions of sexual equality, but its also a response to a divine imperative. Without women, the priesthood is incomplete; with them, it will be deeply enriched. As one liberal Catholic bishop puts it:

I used to think the ordination of women was a serious break with tradition. Of course, in the strict sense it is a break with tradition, but if you see it as a development of tradition, you actually find we are being called to nourish the roots which are often running dry in the Church of England. If priesthood means representing humanity to God and God to humanity, and if you think that is embodied in a person as Christ's ministry was embodied in a person, in days when an exclusively male leadership has been abandoned in all parts of our community, it is difficult to see how a male-only priesthood can truly represent humanity to God and God to humanity because the whole perception of what humanity means has changed. The landscape is different.

But what of the underlying psychological and emotional causes of opposition to women priests? To the opponents, the repulsion felt by a significant number of men and women to the very notion of women preists is a recognition of deep truths divinely embedded in the human soul. To some proponents, it is an expression of unhealthy sexual anxieties. Comments from women campaigners have typically included 'men are afraid we want to rip off their balls' or 'the only difference between them and us is that they have penises'. In keeping with the post-Freudian times, the 1966 report reflected the assumption that subconscious, sexual motivations were at the core of much human behaviour. Some in the Church may have even hoped that people's prejudices could be analysed out of existence if they were, metaphorically, laid bare on the psychiatrist's couch. The suspicion that fear of castration or penis envy were a root cause of the prejudices underlying the debate was expressed in a supplementary essay in the report by one of the commission's members, Dr Robert Hobson, a psychiatrist at the Maudsley hospital. Much of the repugnance and horror evinced by opponents at the very idea of women priests was associated 'with disturbing experiences of the mother during infancy and childhood', he wrote. Women in positions of power might arouse 'anxiety and aggressive sensations'. Men also held in awe and fear such feminine functions as menstruation and childbirth. 'Some fantasies are reminiscent of the myths of the Mother Goddess who embodied not only the fruitful and creative, but the destructive and death-dealing,' said Hobson. While a woman might demand ordination because of her resentment of a man's 'bodily features' and social prestige, a man who has conscious or unconscious anxiety about castration 'often feels threatened by women and compensates for his fears by contempt, treating the female sex as if they were maimed men.' Moreover, men who envied the ability of women to have babies might find refuge in the 'motherly aspects' of priesthood and such 'feminine' expression as ceremonial or ritual dress. Those women who were opposed to the ordination of their own sex were deemed to have accepted their 'fate' – anatomical and social inferiority – and repressed their guilt at wanting to be otherwise by exaggerating their femininity. Such women, Hobson argued, resented those who wanted the priesthood because they threatened the 'roundabout symbolic satisfaction of incestuous desires, which can be achieved in the relationship with a father-priest'.

Another essay writer, Dr Demant, the Regius Professor of Moral and Pastoral Theology at Oxford and one of the leading opponents of women priests of his day, would no doubt have made a perfect case study for Hobson. The sexual chemistry between men and women was potentially explosive in a Church setting, wrote Demant. 'Where women perform personal service as secretaries to businessmen or assistants to professional ones, in a setting where privacy is long and frequent, erotic factors come into play leading, if not frequently, to adultery and fornication, at least often to possessiveness and heart-breaks.' Moreover, he added, male members of the congregation could find themselves sexually attracted to females at the altar, a comment that stung one feminist commentator into the ascerbic rejoinder that the Church was no strip club and a cassock was no G-string.

But the reservations that were harboured by the leadership of the Church of England – and there were many – were not present in all parts of the world. In Hong Kong, Hall had adopted a low profile since his severe reprimand from his fellow bishops but was once again nurturing plans to promote the cause. From the mid-1960s, he was grooming two women deacons for the priesthood, Jane Hwang, vicar of one of the colony's largest parishes, and Joyce Bennett, the daughter of a London master butcher who had been sent to Hong Kong by the Church Missionary Society. Hall confided to Bennett that his mistake in 1944 was that he had only ordained one female candidate. In 1966, in one of his last acts before his retirement, he sent the two women on a world tour as part of an exercise to soften up opinion in the rest of the Anglican Church. When the pair arrived in England, Bennett found she had been invited to preach in a church in Oxfordshire by the rural dean. As both women had been informed before the trip by the then Bishop of Portsmouth, who oversaw women's issues in the Church of England, that they could not operate here as in Hong Kong, Bennett did not don her deacon's robes. 'When I got there, the rural dean, who had seen my robes in photographs, asked where they were,' she recalled recently. 'I told him the Bishop of Portsmouth doesn't allow it. He said, what is the Bishop of Portsmouth to do with me. Please wear them this evening. So I wore them.' After that, Bennett held a discreet meeting with senior figures in the CMS – which was sponsoring her tour – who reluctantly agreed she could wear her robes if asked by the vicar. 'After that I wore my robes everywhere and didn't go to the Bishop of Portsmouth's diocese.'

The mood of the Church of England in general, however, remained unreceptive to the idea of female ordination. When its General Assembly – the immediate forerunner of the General Synod – debated the *Women in Holy Orders* report in February 1967, the pro-women lobby expressed their growing impatience, but time ran out before a vote on the motion calling for women's ordination could be reached. Some proponents of women priests demanded an end to the 'shilly-shallying', while others, including Ellison, stressed the need to proceed with caution in order not to prejudice the delicate unity talks. Ramsey's comment during the debate, if somewhat flippant, displayed his continuing scepticism. 'I am not in sympathy with the ordination of women,' he told the assembly, 'because I think that if God had meant his Church to have women priests, he would have made it known rather sooner than he has done.' When the motion was further debated in July, it was easily rejected after the bishops argued that the Church should wait until the Lambeth Conference had expressed its mind the following year.

The deliberations of the 1968 Lambeth Conference were closely scrutinized, particularly in Hong Kong. Clearly tuned into the *Zeitgeist*, the 460 bishops who gathered at Lambeth Palace had, for the first time, left their gaiters at home. Their sartorial boldness was not matched, however, by decisiveness; the conference found itself unable either to endorse or to reject the principle of ordaining women as priests. Instead, it resorted to that tried and tested principle of Anglicanism, ambiguity. But if the conference did not open the door to the ordination of women priests, it certainly lifted the latch. More damagingly, it left open the question of 'authority' – whether the Anglican Church could or should embark on such a significant change to Christian tradition unilaterally. The conference preparatory committee on women priests, which was chaired by Donald Coggan, said it could find no conclusive theological reasons for debarring women from the priesthood. But there was fierce debate when the issue was considered by the full conference. One bishop said the issue had been introduced like a 'confidence trick'. Trevor Huddleston, who was later to find fame in the anti-apartheid movement, said his diocese in Africa had not even begun discussing the issue because it had better things to do, and asked for more time. Some of the most macho noises emanated from Australia and particularly that conservative Evangelical bastion, Sydney. The then Archbishop, Marcus Loane, angered his liberal colleagues by commenting that the advent of women priests would be 'the death knell of the appeal of the Church to man'. It was just a plain fact, he added, that men could do some things that women could not, and vice versa. Coggan, who was himself an Evangelical, but who was fiercely in favour of women priests, said there were clearly 'further areas of prejudice and ignorance' which still needed breaking down. When his remarks were greeted by some with laughter, a distinct note of exasperation entered his retort. 'This is no joking matter,' he admonished. 'Due to original sin, they are precisely the sort of things which we as bishops are loath to face.'

The most significant contribution, however, was made by Bishop Gilbert Baker, who had succeeded Hall in Hong Kong in 1966 and taken up where his predecessor had left off over the issue of women priests. Under the seemingly deferential guise of asking the guidance of his brother bishops, Baker asked whether he could ordain women as priests. 'I have no desire whatever to go ahead or act in any kind of unilateral way,' he added. The conference, while failing to give an unequivocal 'yes' to Baker, unwittingly left the way clear for him to act. Its final resolution – carried by a show of hands – declared there were no conclusive theological arguments either for or against ordaining women, and called on the separate Anglican provinces to examine the issue and submit their findings to the newly-established Anglican Consultative Council. Provinces were further asked to consult the council before making any decision on ordaining women. Most bishops reasonably assumed that no branch of the worldwide Church would proceed until the period of examination had been completed – a process expected to take a number of years – but the resolution failed to make this sufficiently clear, and proponents of female ordination were not slow to exploit the loophole. It was yet another example of how the structures of the Church proved all too fallible in dealing with such crucial issues.

4

The Philadelphia Incident
(1970–74)

By the beginning of 1970, Michael Ramsey was telling David Frost
in a television interview that he believed 'all Churches' would in
time ordain women to the priesthood, and that a woman would one
day succeed him to the chair of St Augustine. It was a sign of how
much the scene had shifted, however surreptitiously, over the
previous decade. The women's movement had a public face in the
form of the Anglican Group for the Ordination of Women, but
much went on at a subterranean level. Women who felt they had
genuine vocations smouldered with a sense of privation, and subli-
mated their energies into campaigning. Others turned their anger
against men. 'Every deaconess lived with the tension of not being
able to do the whole job,' explains Deaconess Diana McClatchey,
one of the most sagacious veterans of the campaign. 'It was an
absurdity and an injustice. The iron entered their souls.' But their
rage was tempered by caution: they knew progress must be stealthy.
The argued their case at public meetings up and down the country,
chipping away at the old certainties. Confident that they held the
moral high ground, their strategy was to embarrass the bishops into
action. Unlike their counterparts in the United States, who overtly
linked their campaign with the black rights campaign, the movement in England favoured the subtler approach of 'infiltration', of
ensuring women achieved increasingly responsible positions within
the Church structures until their work became indispensable. Once
they had clambered up one step, they would move on to tackling the
next. All but the most militant were wary of putting their heads far

above the parapet. Even Dr Una Kroll, the most outspoken of them, spoke of the 'inbred psychological difficulty' women experienced in admitting they yearned for the priesthood. 'It took me 25 years to gather the courage to say this openly,' she confessed, as if her experience paralleled that of a homosexual coming out of the closet. During the early 1970s, events abroad fuelled a new impetus, a new confidence that victory was within reach. But it was to prove a false and bitter dawn.

Their opponents, meanwhile, were barely conscious of the erosion of their positions. Privately they may have felt threatened, but publicly they expressed few feelings either way towards the women pressing for ordination. Why should they? The issue for them did not concern such emotive questions as justice and women's liberation; those were matters which should properly be confined to the secular sphere. Nor should argument sink to the level of the personal desires of individuals. Those women who believed they were in receipt of God-given vocations were, sadly, self deluding. For the opponents, the only important question centred on how God wished to order his creation. Their view that this precluded women priests was shared by the majority of the Church of England. All they were doing, after all, was to conform to the unbroken tradition of Christendom. They were not the innovators: they could not conceive that they might be forced out of the Church to which they had, in good faith, devoted their lives. Their vision of the Church was, they felt sure, built on theological granite. They had little inkling that it was turning to sand beneath their feet.

In the late 1960s and early 1970s, battles over liturgical reform and the Anglican-Methodist unity scheme absorbed the energies of the Anglo-Catholics. The unity scheme, an attempt to reunite the two Churches which were so close in many ways, had been vigorously opposed by the Anglo-Catholics (the then Bishop of Willesden, Graham Leonard, among them), partly because it would have entailed the Church of England recognizing the validity of female Methodist ministers. The scheme nevertheless had the backing of most of the church leadership including Ramsey. It was scuppered, amid much acrimony, in 1972. Traditionalists like Geldard, who became involved in the Church Union, the oldest

Anglo-Catholic pressure group, still assumed they could hold back the feminist tide with a wall of academic pamphlets and articles. But within a few years, they would switch their tactics, and mobilize their forces in the General Synod in an attempt to stem the flood with their block vote. 'At some point, we realized that it takes a generation to educate people through pamphlets, and we hadn't got a generation to do it.' Like a slumbering dinosaur, the full weight of the opposition to women priests was slow to stir.

Even the decision of the Anglican Consultative Council in 1971 to give the green light to any Anglican province which wished to ordain women priests, failed to wake the traditionalists. A remarkably ill-conceived body, the council consisted of 55 members presided over by the Archbishop of Canterbury; lay men and women drawn from all parts of the world sat alongside bishops as equals. But the council was far from representative. A significant number of its members held only junior posts within their own churches, yet momentous decisions were approved by simple majority votes. In theory, the ACC – as its name suggested – was merely consultative (as was the Lambeth Conference). But in the absence of any authoritative pan-Anglican body, its decisions were seized on as decisive by those who agreed with them. Keen to establish its radical credentials, one of its first acts was to ratify a controversial World Council of Churches decision to allocate nearly £100,000 to organizations representing oppressed racial groups, including black guerrilla movements in Africa.

When the council came to examine the issue of women priests, opinion was sharply divided. Given that only eight of the 21 provinces had by then even begun to act on the Lambeth Conference recommendation that all the churches study the issue of women priests – and none had sent the results of their study – the council could have justifiably deferred a vote until its next meeting two years later. Indeed, few observers thought it would do more than encourage greater research and study. But once again, the radical voice proved the loudest. The matter had been brought up by Baker under the Lambeth Conference resolution asking national churches or provinces to seek and consider the advice of the council before proceeding with the ordination of women. The diocese of

Hong Kong, although tiny by Church of England standards, had been isolated from the rest of the Chinese Church by the communist take-over and found itself in the unique position of being free-standing, and its synod had voted in favour of ordaining women. Baker was nevertheless anxious to consult, particularly as all the other parts of the Anglican Church in South East Asia were opposed.

A flavour of what was an extraordinary meeting has been provided by one of the council members, Irene Jeffreys from Australia. In a letter to Joyce Bennett, she recalled that the debate had begun with a number of bishops declaring their opposition. 'One of the laymen, who was a substitute for an African and is an Englishman engaged in lay training in Uganda, enunciated what so many believe, that you must have a "paternal" figure presiding at the Eucharist, and being the head, the same as the husband/father must be head of his household,' wrote Miss Jeffreys.

> He said his wife had her place and he had his as her head, and inferred that God must be masculine. He apologized to me for saying these things in the presence of a lady, but he could not help his instincts. I said I did not mind but I had my instincts too, and that surely God is in himself both masculine and feminine if he is the creator of all. The Lebanese layman got a little weary of the young man's insistence on the paternal figure and said ironically, 'I suppose you think that God has whiskers!' which made us laugh.

The debate then swung the other way, with a number of speakers pitching in in favour of women priests. Ramsey, seeing the way things were going, mounted a rearguard action against the move by invoking the holy grail of reunion with Rome, but his attempt proved counter-productive. 'The Archbishop of Canterbury was not in favour and when the final vote was about to be taken tried to get permission for the Roman Catholic observer to have a say about what might be the attitude of the Roman Church if we passed it, but there were cries of point of order that an observer should not be allowed to speak on a voting matter, so he was not,' wrote Miss

Jeffreys. 'Father Hugh Bishop (of the Anglo-Catholic Community of the Resurrection) had raised the bogy that it might separate us more from the Romans but as someone said afterwards, the way the Roman Church is going, they might end up before us in ordaining women.'

In fact, by the end of the debate, the issue had broadened far beyond the preoccupations of the diocese of Hong Kong to embrace the whole Church. On the promptings of the American contingent, the original motion was expanded to say that any bishop who ordained women priests with the permission of his province would find his actions 'acceptable to this council'. Ramsey and the then Primate of Scotland, the chairman of that particular session, were among the heavyweight critics of the resolution eventually proposed by a black American priest and seconded by an American woman seminary teacher. But despite, or possibly because of, their opposition, it squeezed through by the narrowest of margins: 24 votes to 22. By a margin of two votes, the worldwide Anglican Church had been set on a course which was to plunge it into bitter civil war. Ramsey and many others, including his successor but one, Robert Runcie, later agreed that the 1968 Lambeth Conference had been foolish to devolve so much power to the council, and its wings have since been clipped. But the damage had been done. Armed with the council's mandate, Baker returned to Hong Kong still hesitating over whether he should make history. In a series of blunt exchanges over the next few months, Ramsey urged Baker to desist, arguing that the majority at Limuru had been too small and, anyway, the council could hardly be said to speak for the whole Church. But Baker was adamant, saying the Church had been 'a club for men only' for too long. The Hong Kong diocesan synod duly gave final clearance in mid-November. On 28 November 1971, Advent Sunday, in front of a packed congregation and the world's press in St John's cathedral in Hong Kong, Jane Hwang, 54, and Joyce Bennett, 49, were ordained Anglicanism's first official women priests. They were two small pebbles in a smaller pond, but the ripples were felt across the globe.

Although the participants in the ordination ceremony were sincere in their actions, many Anglicans – particularly within the

Church of England – were deeply shocked that such a small and relatively insignificant diocese could take such a step on its own. To many, Baker seemed to be cocking a snook at the establishment; in reality, he was a conscientious and even hesitant man who felt driven to act as he did. But the event precipitated action in other parts of the Anglican Church, such as America, which in turn would add to the pressure on those areas which did not. Women priests were no longer a theory: they were a fact. Hong Kong's action firmly cemented the principle of provincial autonomy; just as the British colonies had begun to assert their independence as the Empire declined, so the former missionary outposts of the Church of England were starting to shed their deferrence to the mother Church.

The central structures of the worldwide Anglican Church began to creak under the strain. They had been conceived at a time of fundamental uniformity between all its constituent churches and were not designed to resolve such a divisive issue. Provincial autonomy had been highly effective in allowing the individual churches freedom to adapt their structures and styles of worship to their particular cultural and social situations without impinging on the core of practices and beliefs which they held in common, and which defined them as Anglicans. But the issue of women priests was no respecter of boundaries; it went to the heart of Anglican practice throughout the world. Once it had been embarked on in one area, it seemed to many to be absurd to deny it in others, even though consensus for change had not been achieved among Anglicans, let alone within Christendom at large. Supporters of the move argued that Anglicans should always be open to the genuine promptings of the Holy Spirit. Change is not always tidy: one man's fragmentation is another man's diversity. The ordination of women, they felt, should be seen as an experiment. If it had divine approval, it would spread; if not, it would die out. For Ramsey and his successors, however, such a cavalier attitude towards Church order and discipline was a recipe for anarchy; they were charged with maintaining order in a painfully torn Church without the means to enforce it.

As Robert Runcie recalls:

The Anglican Consultative Council was set up in an untidy way. There are two sources of authority in the Anglican worldwide Church, the authority that comes from the whole body of baptized believers and the authority which comes from ordination and consecration. It did seem to me that the council was set up and acted as if authority simply came from being elected to some central body. This was a democratically defensible position but did not square with that part of authority which belongs to the ordained ministry, whose business it is to listen to what God is saying to the whole body, and to articulate the faith and the discipline of the Church.

Late in the day, the traditionalists in the Church of England would comprehend the significance of what had happened. As one put it:

English Anglicans tend to feel that it is what England does that matters, and to some extent that is true. The fact that two women were ordained in a strange outpost of the Empire on the other side of the world seemed irrelevant. But it wasn't irrelevant to the people who wanted it. In retrospect, it was the thin end of the wedge.

In the Church of England, the argument was about to move into a new arena. The establishment of the General Synod in 1970 – to replace the General Assembly – made a significant impact on the decision-making structures of the Church, centralizing them as never before. Under the old system, the bishops and clergy met separately from the laity, which was denied the vote on certain crucial matters. In the name of democracy, and because the Established Church was obliged to have its legislation approved by Parliament and enshrined in the law of the land, the General Synod brought the three elements together; but in strengthening the muscle of the clergy and laity, the influence of the bishops was diluted. Like Parliament, this structure laid the Church increasingly open to the influence and pressures of the secular society around it. In contrast to Parliament, it was easily characterized by critics as talking shops for those with the time and inclination.

The General Synod, which met three times a year – twice in Church House and once, residentially, on the redbrick campus of York University – soon found itself divided into three groupings – Evangelical, Anglo-Catholic and the open group (liberals) – apparently mirroring the Church at large. In fact, it was a distorted image because it gave undue prominence to the activists; the vast bulk of the Church remained apathetic and even distrustful. But with its quasi-Parliamentary procedures, the synodical system did at least keep the extremists in balance. As soon as the liberals began gaining influence out of proportion to their numbers, the conservatives, particularly the Anglo-Catholics, learnt how to apply the breaks. The General Synod's influential Standing Committee, its 'Cabinet', whose membership reflected the broad spectrum of opinion, was often riven by tension and personality clashes, mirroring in microcosm the struggles that were being fought out in the wider Church. Over the women priests issue there was little meeting of minds on the Committee, and the tactical manoeuverings of both sides became so intense that trivial disputes over Synod procedure often became full-scale battles of will. Synod officers, supposedly neutral civil servants, also wielded substantial power. A bishop who was anxious to speak in a Synod debate, for example, was advised to have a quiet word with a friendly senior official if he wished to ensure he was called.

It was soon to become clear to many that the General Synod did not provide the ideal framework in which an issue as sensitive and subtle as the ordination of women as priests could be discussed with cool heads. Both sides realized that it was essentially a case of 'winner takes all', and neither side was above discreet manipulation of the system or using procedure to frustrate their enemies. But important legal and theological questions were also raised. Could, or should, fundamental questions of doctrine be settled – and 2,000 years of tradition swept aside – by a Parliamentary-style division on a dull afternoon in November? There were those who found the whole concept of such an issue being determined in the same way as the future of the parson's freehold or the Church's stance on South Africa absurd. Traditionalists sometimes argued (usually when they were losing the debate) that the General Synod had no legal or moral authority to make such a far-reaching decision. But the various attempts to challenge the scope of the Synod's powers in the courts failed. The progressives, meanwhile, pointed out that synodical government was a distinguishing mark of the Anglican Church, and the guiding influence of the Holy Spirit could surely operate as effectively in its committee rooms and debating chamber as in the defining councils of the early Church. Moreover, any legislation to permit the ordination of women would have to be decided under the tough provisions of 'Article 8' business. This would require it to leap some very high hurdles indeed; without strong backing throughout the Church as a whole it would stand little chance of ultimate success.

George Austin was one of the few Anglo-Catholic candidates in the first election to the Synod in 1970 to include in his manifesto that he was opposed to women priests. Austin had been a close observer of the situation in the Church of Sweden where the ordination of women priests had initially been a disaster. The Church of Sweden was Lutheran but it had many affinities with the Church of England, including the office of bishops. It was also an 'established' church; indeed, its clergy are employees of the State. The progressive Swedish government found itself faced with the embarrassing fact that it was permitting discrimination against women within its own administrative ranks. While women's organizations from across the political spectrum united to agitate for change, resistance grew among the clergy, many of whom were influenced by Anglo-Catholic theology. As early as the 1950s, Sweden proved a testing ground for many of the arguments for and against women priests. In 1957, legislation to ordain women was presented to the Swedish Church Assembly by the government, but was thrown out. The rejection so shocked the country that the government, amid charges of unconstitutionality, dissolved the assembly and had another one elected, which duly endorsed the legislation. The first women priests were ordained in 1960, but the Church was brought to the brink of schism and initially lost more male priests than it gained female ones. Young male priests who refused to work alongside women ministers found their promotions blocked; some of the women priests even found themselves shunned by former liberal allies who opposed the interference of the State. The hatreds ran deep and the resentment still lingers today. As Austin puts it: 'I saw the unpleasantness and persecutions of my friends over there. I had seen it was on the way over here.'

The Swedish debacle was one of the areas covered in a sweeping 1972 report compiled by Christian Howard, an impressively even-handed production given the pro-ordination bias of its author. Like all such reports, it was a forensic analysis of the positions of both sides rather than an attempt to resolve the argument because, as Howard (a descendant of Catherine Howard, the fifth wife of Henry VIII) pointed out, the gulf between the two was so great that they could not even agree on what could be included as evidence in the debate. But the semi-official report rekindled the debate. Howard's personal reaction to receiving Communion at the hands of a woman priest at two different services in Sweden, which she had visited while researching the 85-page document, would have made Austin squirm. 'At one service, I looked up from my prayer book and saw a woman in vestments with a rather nice hairdo. I did a double-take!' she told one newspaper. 'But the second was such a corporate thing, she seemed to sink into the whole and the fact that she was a woman seemed unimportant.' In 1972, the General Synod voted to take note of the report, and in July 1973 two motions were considered and subsequently referred to the individual dioceses to sound out opinion before they were brought back to the Synod in 1975.

As the date for the first full-scale Synod confrontation over women priests loomed, women were consolidating their positions. A phalanx – if not a monstrous regiment – of powerful women had taken their place in Synod, including Howard and Betty Ridley, the Third Church Estates Commissioner (a senior officer of the Church Commissioners, the Church's financial arm). In 1971, the Synod had widened the scope of the Church's 80 deaconesses, giving them permission to lead worship, preach, assist at Communion, baptize and bury the dead; many women felt they could not be far from achieving the priesthood. In 1974, as if to ram home the point, the Methodist Church fell into line with the other Free Churches and ordained 24 women ministers. Pressure was also exerted from another, more secular quarter. Parliament began debating a Bill designed to end discrimination against women in society at large, particularly in the area of employment. A number of MPs and peers argued that the churches should not be granted an exemption – the liberal peer Baroness Seear argued that women would otherwise have to wait until 'eternity' to be ordained priests. Had they prevailed, the male-only priesthood would have been made illegal in a stroke. But even supporters of women priests campaigned over the next few years against an exemption for the Churches. They felt they were close to a breakthrough anyway, and were deeply conscious of the turmoil caused in the Church of Sweden when the State imposed women clergy. In the event, the provisions of the Sex Discrimination Act 1975 did not apply to organized religion. Other branches of the worldwide Anglican Church were way ahead of them.

The American branch, the Episcopal Church, had been deeply coloured by the radicalism of the 1960s: the anti-Vietnam riots, the black rights movement and the rise of militant feminism had all left their mark on its leadership. Although still a favoured nest for America's elite Wasps (white Anglo-Saxon Protestants) – the former president George Bush is a prominent member – the public profile of the two-hundred-year-old Church was undergoing a radical shift. Until then, the exclusion of women from positions of authority was largely unquestioned; only men could become deputies (delegates) on the National Convention, the Episcopal Church's equivalent of the General Synod. But by the end of the decade, as the cause of equal rights for women took off in secular society, there was growing agitation for the ordination of women as priests and bishops. At the same time, other liberal agendas were being actively pursued. Left-wing political causes were espoused, and grants donated to militant organizations including the Black Panthers. The frontiers of sexual ethics had also been pushed back, and the Church was the first to ordain openly practising homosexuals.

To its critics, the American Episcopal Church represents all that is worst about liberal Anglicanism. In their eyes, its efforts to become 'relevant' resulted in the dilution of its essential message. Its espousal of ephemeral, secular causes led it to become shallow and ultimately unsatisfactory for many of its traditional adherents.

The liberal 'takeover', the critics point out, coincided with a sharp decline in membership. Between the late 1960s and the late 1980s, numbers dropped by more than a million to two and a half million, leading the Library of Congress in Washington to demote the Episcopal Church from the status of a 'denomination' to that of a 'sect'. This was happening during a period when churchgoing in America was undergoing a revival (though other mainstream American Churches were also losing numbers). While the liberals have been undeniably successful in rendering the Church more accessible to minority groups, members of those groups have hardly rushed to sign up. Church of England traditionalists have not been slow to point out that American trends usually take a decade or so to cross the Atlantic. An even more fundamental charge levelled against the liberals is that, in their anxiety to maintain TC (theological correctness), they are profoundly intolerant of those who disagree with them: that charity, in other words, does not begin at home. Opponents of the ordination of women priests in America feel they have been dealt a very raw deal. Not only has there been a slow haemorrhage of members, but there have been a series of public splits which have further undermined the authority of the Church.

This turmoil was still in the future when the issue of the ordination of women was first considered at the 1970 convention in Houston, Texas. A resolution declaring that women should be admitted to all the orders, deacons, priests and bishops, narrowly failed to achieve a majority. By the 1973 convention in Louisville, the bishops as a group had voted in favour of ordaining women, the Anglican Consultative Council had signalled a green light and the proponents felt that they were a hair's breadth from victory. But in the intervening three years, the opposition had mobilized, fuelled by a backlash provoked by the controversial revision of the traditional prayer-book. After a fierce debate in the convention at Louisville, the resolution calling on the Episcopal Church to rewrite its laws to allow women to be ordained was defeated. Although a majority had voted in favour, so-called 'divided' votes – the equivalent of abstentions – were counted against under the rules. The vote was: clerical, 50 in favour, 43 against and 20 divided; lay, 49, in favour, 37 against and 26 divided.

Many of the opponents, who had initially been caught theologically unprepared, were by then vocal and passionate, deploying the argument that God's relationship with his Church – as initiator and receiver – was analogous to that of a man and a woman. Therefore, only males, the initiators in biological and psychological terms, could truly represent Christ at the altar. Some used overtly sexual imagery, describing male priests as symbols of the 'seminal initiative of God', a view which infuriated supporters of women priests. McClatchey recalls: 'The argument I had to come to terms with was the symbolism of the Church as the bride of Christ. But I was deeply offended by reading an article by an American priest who saw the divine initiative in terms of the sexual initiative, a divine semen being transmitted to the believer.' The result of Louisville was a body blow to the proponents of women priests; forty bishops issued a statement calling it an abuse of moral justice. It had a personal effect on some. Janet Watrous was so horrified by the Louisville convention that she dropped out of her theological college, and she was far from being the only one. 'The discord was unbelievable,' she said. 'While there, I was introduced as a seminary student to one man who blatantly refused to shake hands with me. I had never met personal rejection like that. And then there was that horrible moment when the motion for women's ordination was defeated. It was like dying!'

The front-line campaigners were sharply divided about how to proceed. The moderate faction was convinced that a more sophisticated political strategy would eventually secure victory; the militants declared, in the terminology of revolution, that the 'democratic process, the political dynamics, and the legal guidelines' were 'out of step with the divine imperative which says, now is the time'. They did not wait long. On a sweltering July day in 1974, on the feast of St Mary and St Martha, eleven women ranging in age from 27 to 79 were ordained priests in contravention of Church law. The Philadelphia eleven as they were to become known – the illegal ceremony was staged in the Church of the Advocate in the 'city of brotherly love' – adopted a stridently feminist posture, which seemed consciously designed to cause maximum provocation among opponents. In a joint statement, the women said: 'Our primary motivation is to begin to free the priesthood from the bondage it suffers as long as it is characterized by categorical exclusion of persons on the basis of sex. We are fully aware of the risks to ourselves and others but we must be true to our vocations.' But, as usual in the American context, the civil rights cause was also in the background. The rector of the church was black, as was the cross-bearer at the head of the procession, who was destined to surface 14 years later in an even more controversial guise. Then an executive for an oil company, her name was Barbara Harris. Despite this, the majority of the women – who were ordained by three retired bishops and one active bishop flown in from Costa Rica – were white and from middle-class backgrounds. One, Nancy Wittig, grew up in an episcopalian household, the daughter of a career naval officer.

> 'I read Mary Daly's *Beyond God the Father* in the summer of 1974,' she said later. 'That book empowered me; it made me literally get up from the comfortable, safe, quiet country couch where I had been reading and say, "Now I know what I am supposed to do. It is time for the Church to move and to be changed, and if there is any way I can have a part of it, that is what my responsibility is." It was that clear, that firm, that definite.'

The irregular ordinations were met with a wail of dismay by Episcopalian traditionists. The ceremony itself was disrupted when five priests, led by the Revd Charles Osborn of the conservative American Church Union, strode up the aisle denouncing the proceedings as a 'perversion' and, in less than flattering imagery, accusing the bishops of trying to 'make stones into bread'. In Kansas City, a priest flew the American flag from his church at half mast and upside down. 'This was the only way I could think of to show my personal disgust,' he said. 'Women cannot be validly ordained any more than you can validly consecrate Coca Cola and potato chips in place of wine and bread. I myself prefer scotch to wine, but I can't put that on the altar and call it the blood of Christ.' Meanwhile, Americans transfixed by the travails of President

Nixon – who was facing impeachment following the Watergate scandal – had their attention momentarily diverted by the prospect of its ecclesiastical equivalent, the deposing of a bishop. In advance of the ceremony, the presiding bishop, Dr John Allin, had appealed to the mutinous bishops to abandon their plans until the Church had come to a common mind on the issue, and warned the women involved that though their ordinations might be theologically valid – because of the 'laying on of hands' – they would not be recognized as legal. Afterwards Allin, who felt there was no excuse for such indiscipline, called an emergency meeting of all the 111 bishops which was held at the O'Hare International Tower, a hotel at Chicago airport. Many Church leaders felt the maverick quartet of bishops should be deposed to deter other potential rebels. In fact, only Bishop Antonio Ramos of Costa Rica (the others being retired) was required to explain his actions, but at the end of the day, the complexity of the deposition process and a lack of will-power among the bishops combined to ensure the incident fizzled out. Somewhat half-heartedly, the bishops declared that the 'necessary conditions' for valid ordinations had not been present at Philadelphia, and they voted to 'decry' the actions of the four who presided. Within a few months, however, they had reiterated their support for the principle of the ordination of women by 97 votes to 65, with six abstentions. When four more women were irregularly ordained in Washington in September the following year, there was barely a bleat of protest.

5

False Starts

(1975–79)

The 1975 General Synod represented a watershed in the life of the Church of England, determining its course for the next decade. But while it was the occasion that irrevocably put the ordination of women at the heart of the Church's agenda, the motion approved by the Synod was the cause of much bad blood: ill conceived and illiberal, it cast a blight over the way the controversy was handled for many years.

By the time the matter reached the floor of the Synod, the Church had acquired a new Archbishop of Canterbury. In contrast to his predecessor, there was no doubt where Donald Coggan stood on the question of women's ordination. A bespectacled, middle-class Evangelical, he had displayed his pro-women credentials at the 1968 Lambeth Conference. His passion shone through in a sermon he delivered while Archbishop of York at Whitby, the community founded by that seventh-century example of female emancipation St Hilda. 'How long can you cripple the Church by letting your women do little more than provide the food after parish functions, mend the linen, clean the brasses (all good deeds) and otherwise serve as parish workers, but not entrust them on a big scale?' he implored his fellow churchmen. His impact was to be limited, however. Appointed to Canterbury in May 1974 aged 64, he could look forward to no more than five years in office; even the most optimistic doubted that women could be ordained within his tenure.

As the date of the Synod approached, the Church's mood became increasingly erratic as the propaganda engines of both sides were cranked into action. In what was interpreted as a direct challenge to Coggan, the Anglo-Catholics issued a polemic restating their classic position that Anglicans lacked the authority unilaterally to depart from Christian tradition. Meanwhile, a few weeks before the debate, supporters of women's ordination pulled off the first of many publicity coups when a group of parishioners from a progressive East London parish handed in a petition to the Bishop of Southwark, Mervyn Stockwood, demanding the ordination as a priest of Elsie Baker, who had served as a deaconess for 33 years (and had already surreptitiously conducted the occasional wedding at her church). The parishioners, from Blackheath, said they shared her conviction that she had a genuine vocation to be a priest. While they realized the gesture was futile (though it achieved substantial publicity), the pro-ordination camp had already grasped the power of illustrating their case through sympathetic human examples. Their opponents found it difficult to argue against a woman who insisted that she had been called by God to become a priest; they could hardly deny it outright, so they were reduced, weakly, to arguing that she might be mistaken or that, even if she wasn't, she must ignore it. Of the 93 deaconesses then active in the Church, all but ten felt they had vocations to the priesthood.

The edginess was compounded by a series of errors of judgement perpetrated in the run-up to the 1975 debate. The General Synod's Standing Committee had drafted two resolutions to be decided by all 43 diocesan synods to determine whether a consensus existed for change before the matter returned for national debate. The first asked diocesan synods whether they agreed that there were 'no fundamental objections' to the ordination of women; if this motion was approved, they were further asked whether the Church should begin the process of removing 'legal or other barriers' to ordination. Once opinion had thus been measured at grass roots level, it was thought, these two motions would form the basis for the national debate in General Synod.

But the wording of the first motion was gravely flawed. It implied that a synod, by waving the magic wand of a majority vote, could dispel the centuries-old theological objections to women priests into thin air as if they had never existed. This was a vain hope. If passed, therefore, the motion would unrealistically raise the expectations of the advocates of women priests who argued that, once the principle had been agreed, it was a small step to embrace the second motion. In the event, however, members of diocesan synods were prepared to look but not to leap. The voting patterns revealed a groundswell of support for the principle of female ordination but a characteristic hesitancy about putting it into practice. The hopes of senior officials that the second motion would gain the support of at least half the diocesan synods, enabling them to bring it to the General Synod, were dashed. While 30 recorded no 'fundamental objections' to the ordination of women priests, only 15 (just over a third) approved the drawing up of legislation to make it a reality.

This left the standing committee in a quandary, and it panicked. In a hurried and heavy-handed directive, it recommended that the second motion should not be debated at all in the Synod on the grounds that the Church at large clearly lacked the will power to translate principle into practice. Committee members feared a backlash if the first motion was passed and the second fell. But many Synod members were furious; the directive seemed to them an unwarranted encroachment on their freedom of action. Meanwhile, supporters of women priests attacked the committee for its caution, contrasting what they saw as its cravenness with the attitude of more progressive parts of the Anglican Church; four Anglican provinces – Burma, Canada, the Indian Ocean and New Zealand – had by then decided to press ahead, and three women had already been lawfully ordained priests in Hong Kong.

Thus, when the Synod convened on the campus of York university in July, passions were running high (if largely buttoned up behind clerical cassocks). In the debate, the supporters, led by Kenneth Woollcombe, the then Bishop of Oxford, stressed that the humanity of Christ was more important than his particular gender, and a male-only priesthood was becoming increasingly unrepresentative. The opponents, spearheaded by the donnish Eric Kemp, Bishop of Chichester and father figure of the Anglo-Catholic movement, and Graham Leonard, by then Bishop of Truro, countered that the Church of England, a tiny part of Western Christianity, neither should nor could act unilaterally. Leonard said that to ordain women could be to criticize God for having created two distinct sexes. Coggan made a powerful speech in favour, declaring in Churchillian rhetoric: 'This could be the Church's finest hour.' He said that no very clearly defined or rigid pattern of ministry had evolved by the first century. The pattern of the three-fold ministry had emerged 'by a process of Spirit-guided evolution, rather than by a divine dictate of the Master of the Church.' Many doctrinal insights, he continued, were unknown to the early Christians, but had been brought to the Church down the centuries by the Holy Spirit. 'It causes me very great and very deep anxiety. Supposing by the very nature of our response we are blocking the promptings of the Holy Spirit? How long can we keep doing this?'

At the end of the debate, the first motion – 'that this Synod considers that there are no fundamental objections to the ordination of women' – was carried in all three Houses, though only by a majority of 14 in the House of Clergy. When members turned to the second issue, chaos ensued. An alternative second motion, proposed by a representative of the standing committee, which said that the 'time was not right' to remove the barriers to women priests was thrown out, having been lost in the House of Laity. But the opposite motion, that the barriers should be removed, was also lost, this time in the Houses of Bishops and Clergy. The General Synod eventually kicked the issue into touch (a favourite tactic employed on numerous occasions) by approving a compromise motion which charged the bishops to determine the appropriate time to return to the issue. It was a perfect example of the deficiencies of the Synod when it came to debating such an issue. Almost as an afterthought, and despite the arguments advanced during the debate that the views of other Christian Churches should not influence its decisions, the Synod also called for efforts to involve the Roman Catholic and Orthodox Churches in an urgent 're-examination' of their opposition to women priests. Some in the Church of England hoped, in a bout of wishful thinking, that their ecumenical partners would see the error of their ways and fall in meekly behind them. Unfortunately, as they were to discover, the other Churches had little time for the way Anglicans made their decisions.

For the Anglo-Catholics, the debate was a rude awakening. George Austin recalls:

> It was no longer the case that proponents of women priests had to acknowledge and respect the views of those who disagreed, because the Synod had ruled out any objections. I believe that the vote was the cause of the bitterness up to 1988, when the Bishops produced their report which said there were different points of view. Between those times there was very little theological debate of any consequence and the possibility of dismissing us as misogynists, as repressed homosexuals, grew apace through that period. The unpleasantness and the unchristian nature of the argument fed on the improper motion. I don't think we saw the significance of it immediately. It was only afterwards that we realized that, from that moment on, we were marginalized. It suddenly became possible for the opponents not to have to use theological argument, but to say to us 'you must be daft' or 'if only we can bring you out of your ghetto'. It was a crass motion.

Leonard now says:

> That the Synod could bring itself to pass such a motion almost surpasses comprehension. This was the nadir of Anglican theological thought. The idea that you could actually decide something like this by majority vote was extraordinary. A lot of weight was subsequently put on that motion by supporters of ordination. They referred to it again and again.

From a different perspective, supporters of women priests also came to see the main motion as a mistake, not because it killed rational theological debate – they deny they treated the opposition's arguments any less seriously after the debate than before – but because it gave their opponents a grievance. Runcie recalls: 'It was convenient to the doctrine of a liberal tyranny to suppose that we used it to dismiss theological objections. It did seem to me that, although that debate and vote had taken place, there clearly remained a large number of objections, and I was one who abstained on that motion.' But the defeat of the second motion was an even more bitter pill, and the warnings uttered during the debate that the women priests campaign would be driven underground were borne out with a vengeance.

Within a year, the Church of England was once again finding itself pulled in opposite directions, this time by external forces. In the summer of 1976, both the Eastern Orthodox and the Roman Catholic Churches firmly informed the Church of England that the ordination of women would jeopardize any further convergence of their faiths. Even the Old Catholics – the tiny group which had split from Rome in the last century because it could not stomach the doctrine of papal infallibility but whose orders were conveniently recognized by both Rome and the Anglicans – issued an unambiguous health warning. Like the Old Catholics, the Eastern Orthodox Churches – who had broken with the West 1,000 years before – had a special place in the affections of Anglicans because of their shared suspicions of the centralizing tendencies of Rome. Robert Runcie, then Bishop of St Albans, was one of a group of Anglican leaders who held regular meetings with their Orthodox counterparts, whose spirituality they admired. In reality, however, the gulf between the two Churches was more profound than either side would care to admit. Though both share the concept of 'dispersed' authority – Orthodoxy, like Anglicanism, is a 'fellowship' of autonomous Churches under a nominal head – their view of what this means diverges dramatically: while Orthodoxy has remained steadfastly unreconstructed since medieval times – lack of central authority makes change impractical anyway – Anglicanism's pragmatism is anathema to the bearded patriarchs of Orthodoxy. The issue of women priests crystallized the divergence. At a crucial meeting in Moscow in August 1976, Orthodox leaders, hoping to deter the Anglican Church from admitting women to the priesthood, told the Anglican delegation that such a move would create 'serious obstacles'. The following year, during a visit to Istanbul, Coggan was told by Demetrios I, the Ecumenical Patriarch, that the Orthodox could not countenance 'novelties entirely foreign to the undivided Church and to its faith and tradition'. Coggan replied that Anglicans did not want to impose women priests on the Orthodox; they were just appealing for understanding. But there was little real meeting of minds between the two Churches. Relations reached a crisis at a meeting in Cambridge in 1977, at which one Orthodox bishop, shocked to hear that some parts of the Anglican Church were already ordaining women, stormed out. Runcie, who was leading the Anglican delegation, recalls: 'The bishop – he was a sort of Michael Heseltine of the Orthodox Church – said he had not realized what had been going on, and asked what was the point of carrying on with the discussions. He did not carry the others with him but he sowed a sort of unease.' The Athens statement the following year spelt an end to meaningful progress.

Relations with Rome were equally fraught. Apart from the Anglican distrust of Rome autocracy, the 100-year-old papal declaration (*Apostolicae Curae*) that Anglican orders were 'null and void' remained a source of deep resentment, and a seam of English anti-Catholicism dating from the era of the Armada still ran through the national psyche. Nevertheless, the two faiths had a shared history until the Reformation; though both partners still bore the emotional scars of the bitter ecclesiastical separation, they felt they could make up their differences. A succession of cordial meetings between Archbishops and Popes, and the setting up of the joint ARCIC unity talks – a sort of marriage guidance counselling – seemed to confirm this. Relations at parish level became increasingly friendly, partly driven by the necessity of sharing ever dwindling resources. Anglicans could not avoid the fact that the Roman Catholic Church constituted the largest branch of Christendom, outnumbering them in world terms by more than ten to one.

Acting on the instructions of the Synod, Coggan wrote to Pope Paul informing him of Anglican moves to ordain women. The Pope's response was glacial; such a development would, he replied, introduce 'grave difficulty' into the unity talks between the Churches. He cited the classic Roman Catholic position: that Christ chose only male apostles; that the Church had consistently excluded women from the priesthood; that such a practice was in accordance with God's plan for his Church. There followed another unsatisfactory flurry of correspondence before the publication, in January 1977, of a papal declaration (*Inter Insigniores*) which once again gave a resounding 'no' to the ordination of women. The Roman Catholic Church 'in fidelity to the example of the Lord, does not consider herself authorized to admit women to priestly ordination,' it stated. Meanwhile, a small joint committee was set up to examine the practical difficulties arising from the impasse (the so-called Versailles Consultation). It reported that, though grave, the issue of women priests need not be an insuperable obstacle to eventual union. In the face of these conflicting views, many Anglicans strongly believed that reunion was still achievable by the end of the millennium; some optimists (Runcie was among them) made 1990 their target date.

In reality, the unity signals were constantly being scrambled by the interference caused by the storm over women priests. The grandiose vision of full reunion was kept in view only because a good deal of self deception was practised by both sides. The exchange of letters treated the issue as if it were still in the realm of theory; in fact, women had already been ordained priests within the worldwide Anglican Church. The Anglicans had presented the Roman Catholics with a *fait accompli* and effectively said: take it or leave it. When the Catholics failed to break off unity talks then and there, many Anglicans mistakenly assumed their new partners were prepared to be far more flexible than their negative official stance suggested. But the Vatican was not maintaining relations because it recognized that it might be on the brink of admitting women to the priesthood itself, or because it could see a way of accommodating the Anglican position. The Pope did, however, regard the Church of England as the jewel in the crown of the worldwide Anglican Church; if he could prevent women being ordained there, he believed he could negotiate directly with England and ignore the outposts.

On the Anglican side, there were also serious reservations about reunion, though they were rarely referred to in polite company. A vast reservoir of mutual suspicion still soured relations at many levels, and there were Anglicans who privately suspected Rome was more interested in a take-over than in a partnership between equals. Rome still occupied a special place in Protestant demonology, and many Evangelicals pointed out that, by flirting with papism, they were in danger of relegating their relations with other Protestant Churches. The increasingly influential liberals, meanwhile, were impatient with the stately ritual dance of the unity talks which was hampering the introduction of their own agenda. One liberal Church of England bishop called on Anglicans to ignore the Pope, because if a 'considerable' number of Christians agreed on certain policy, they should pursue it. It was pointed out to him that the word 'considerable' was a relative one; that in global terms, the ordination of women was the goal of a tiny minority. A large number of undecided Anglicans were still swayed by the fear that women priests would destroy the prospects of reunion, but the lack of concrete results over the next decade eroded the force of that argument. Diana McClatchey recalls: 'There was a real tussle of loyalty between those who definitely wanted to see closer links with Rome and those who thought the Church had to take the step of ordaining women. It would have made it much harder for us if Rome had recognized Anglican orders, but nothing happened. I minded about unity but I just did not feel it was a realistic prospect.' From the perspective of people like Graham Leonard, however, the unity process had been derailed not by the intransigence of Rome but by those individual Anglican Churches which had unilaterally ordained women.

America seemed little concerned with such sensitivities. At its 1976 convention in Minneapolis, amid acrimony and dissension, the Episcopal Church once again debated the ordination of women. Despite the desire of many responsible Anglican leaders for the worldwide Church to synchronize its progress on this issue, the Americans were too engrossed in navel gazing to notice the rest of the world. The vote was, however, crucial to the shape of the debate in England; not only was America geographically close but their more militant pro-women campaigners had no qualms about exporting their brash brand of proselytizing across the Atlantic. A 'yes' vote would therefore raise a dangerous new question in England, namely should women priests validly ordained abroad be allowed to operate as priests in this country?

On the afternoon of 16 September, after four hours of emotive debate, the lay and clerical members of the Episcopal Church's General Convention rose to their feet to decide whether they agreed with their bishops, who had voted in favour of women priests the previous day. Pro-women campaigners in the packed public gallery joined hands. One woman said later: 'I don't believe I have ever stood in the midst of such an electrical silence.' Only a simple majority was required, but the result was balanced on a knife edge; the opponents had threatened schism if the result went against them. After the vote, there was a lengthy wait as the ballot papers were counted. Then the result was announced: the resolution had passed, but by the slimmest of margins (the majority among the clergy was six). The reaction – hugs and cheering from the supporters, anger and silence from those opposed – could have been a scene from the aftermath of the Church of England's debate 16 years later. By the end of 1977, about 100 women had been ordained priests, and the fifteen women involved in the illegal ceremonies in Philadelphia and Washington had their ordinations retrospectively recognized. The Revd Susan Hiatt, one of the 'eleven', declared the period of 'guerrilla priesthood' over. Coggan, a guest at the Convention, was clearly delighted. Addressing more than 1,000 members the day after the vote, he said tension was inevitable but, though it could be the cause of bitterness and division, it could also be 'a source of power and beauty and music'. He continued: 'Let me put it this way, that if in the days ahead with these tensions and with these wounds there arises a situation in which you feel unable to put your arms around a person who voted as you thought wrongly and say to him or her "I differ from you but I love you dearly in Christ", then there will be an occasion where deep penitence is called for.' He, like many other proponents of women priests, had seriously underestimated the backlash.

Within hours, the polarization had began. A group of 37 bishops announced they could not ordain women, and the Fellowship of Concerned Churchmen, a coalition of organizations opposing the ordination of women, gave notice that it intended to split from the main body of the Episcopal Church. Its grievances were not limited

to women priests; prayer-book revisions, the ordination of homosexuals and funding for groups like the Black Panthers had all
contributed to a melting pot of dissatisfaction. Over the ensuing
months, a number of parishes withdrew from the mainstream
Church and began to form their own alternative network. At a rebel
congress at St Louis in September 1977, attended by 1,746
Anglicans, a breakaway Church – the Anglican Church of North
America – was formed. But the 'continuing' Church was itself rent
with internal division; its leaders, no longer united by a common
enemy, squabbled and the original body splintered into at least five
new Churches (though by the 1990s, they had largely coalesced
under the banner of the international Traditional Anglican
Communion). In 1985, it was estimated that the total number of
refugees in these splinter groups stood at about 15,000, a tiny
proportion of the Episcopal Church membership. However, this
figure excluded those who remained or those who left organized
religion or those who joined other denominations.

But in the weeks immediately after the 1977 St Louis congress,
the Episcopal Church's bishops were alarmed at the extent of the
secession movement. When they met at Port St Lucie in Florida in
September, they were in some disarray. In his opening address
Bishop John Allin, their presiding bishop, said they needed to find
ways to deal with 'divisions and fragmentations in the Church', a
situation he went on vividly to highlight by admitting that even he
himself was unable to accept women as priests. Though he offered
to resign as presiding bishop, his colleagues rejected his offer and
affirmed 'the right of the presiding bishop to hold a personal
conviction on the issue'. The bishops then went on to produce a
statement on collegiality that recognized 'sharp differences of
conscientious conviction' and upheld the need for sensitivity,
patience and forbearance 'expressed in a willingness to listen, to
communicate and to learn'. In an 'appeal to those who have separated themselves from our Church,' they wrote 'we are certain that
it is not necessary for you to leave the Episcopal Church in order to
live with your Christian conscience and witness.' By the end of
the meeting, many bishops felt they had done enough to preserve
the unity of the Episcopal Church. But dissidents who remained in

the Church soon felt marginalized and discriminated against; for them, the assurances of the bishops were not worth the paper they were written on. Over the next decade many were to depart for the Roman Catholic Church, and about a dozen parishes were given special dispensation to transfer their allegiances in groups, led by their clergy. While the clergy were eventually ordained as Roman Catholic priests, the laity were allowed to carry on using the Anglican liturgy in their worship.

The Church of England, meanwhile, was faced with a dilemma. Until women began being ordained abroad, the tradition within the worldwide Anglican Church had been that an Anglican priest properly ordained and in good standing with his local bishop was automatically regarded as properly ordained throughout the Church, able to celebrate Communion anywhere (with the appropriate local permission). That tradition was broken in November 1976 when the English House of Bishops, acting on advice from its legal advisers, announced that it would forbid any Communion service in any English church if it was intended that a woman priest should preside. Proponents of women priests argued forcibly that, as the trend in the worldwide Church seemed to be in favour of ordaining women, any constituent Church which fell out of step was falling into a kind of schism with the rest. Opponents countered with the argument that it was the foreign Churches which had broken ranks and anyway, as individual Churches were theoretically autonomous, what happened abroad should have no bearing on what happened within the Church of England. Pressure thus came to be exerted on the Church of England which had more to do with the failure of pan-Anglican structures to restrain progressive elements in the worldwide Church than any overwhelming theological consensus on the issue.

The practical implications were felt immediately. Campaigners for the ordination of women in England, who were furious with the bishops for banning women priests from abroad, began to organize illegal services in their own country as part of their efforts to shift the centre of gravity. A string of battle-hardened women ordained in America were imported as 'audio-visual aids' for the cause, but not with unalloyed success. The first in November 1976, a

Communion service celebrated in an east London Unitarian church by Alison Palmer – one of the four women illegally ordained in Washington the previous year – was not welcomed by moderate campaigners, who feared the defiant gesture would prove counter-productive. The opponents were quick to capitalize, with Leonard portraying the service as a misuse of Holy Communion and a provocative attempt to force the hand of the Church of England. And while Coggan made no comment, senior bishops, however sympathetic to the cause, viewed it as misguided and mistimed.

Within a few days, however, another provocative service was staged in the central London church of St Martin in the Fields. Ostensibly a thanksgiving for the ordination of women priests in Canada, it was also a protest at the isolation of the Church of England and *cri de coeur* from women such as Kroll. The sermon was preached by the Bishop of Winchester, John Taylor, and during the service, the unconsecrated bread and wine was offered to Elsie Baker so that she could symbolically indicate that she could not proceed with the service. But in October of the following year, campaigners went even further: at the invitation of two parish priests, Palmer publicly celebrated Communion in two Church of England churches (in Manchester and Newcastle), an unprece-dented act and a blatant breach of ecclesiastical discipline. Her host in Manchester, Alfred Willets, rector of the All Apostles church, and in Newcastle, Ian Harker, vicar of St Thomas the Martyr, were sharply reprimanded by the Archbishops of Canterbury and York but remained unrepentant. At the Manchester service, Willet's wife Phoebe, a deaconess who was mortally ill with cancer, gave the sermon. 'We have spent too many centuries apologizing to Big Brother for being born women,' she said. 'It is about time we stopped crawling under Victorian pews saying we are sorry we exist. Even when, in this church, we have burnt those pews we still create imaginary ones to crawl underneath. It was God's idea that we were created male and female, and it was a glorious idea.' Within a few months, she and her husband were again to breach Church law by publicly (a Government Minister was among the congregation) jointly celebrating communion – not only was she a woman but also a laywoman. It was her last appearance in church before her death.

While these acts of defiance contributed to the mounting fury of the debate, ecclesiastical politics was becoming ever more devious. Geldard remembers how, soon afterwards, Una Kroll tried to embarrass the Church Union of which he had become secretary by applying for membership.

> She had an Anglo–Catholic background and had been a religious sister in South Africa. One group of people wanted the Church Union to say no, those who favour the ordination of women can't become members, but opposition to women priests was not an article of faith. I remember the executive was petrified about how they could say no to her. They realized they had been caught; if they said no, she would make great capital of it, but if they had admitted her, she would exploit it. I remember I gave a memorandum to the executive saying the reason I thought she should not be a member was because she had participated in the service at St Martin in the Fields. I argued that someone who had brought the Eucharist into disrepect is not a person who should be in the Church Union. There was a great sigh of relief.

At one stage in 1977, Kroll, increasingly impatient and disheartened, declared she was withdrawing from the fray because her health was suffering. One friend said: 'She was one of the very few women prepared to speak out and she was very bitter about other women who let her take the flak and waited to benefit from the results.' In fact, Kroll flung herself even more fiercely into the battle, and was a key activist at the crucial Lambeth Conference the following summer, which, for the first time, eschewed the homely discomfort of Lambeth Palace in favour of the sprawling hilltop campus of Kent University overlooking Canterbury and its cathedral – the spiritual heart of the worldwide Church. But spirituality was often at a premium as the 450 bishops (as usual, the Americans were hugely over-represented in relation to the membership of the Episcopal Church) wrangled over a formula which would simultaneously rubber-stamp the actions of those parts of the Church which had already ordained women, while keeping on board those which were opposed or resented the precipitate action of their fellow Anglicans.

Not for the first time, theologians and bishops found themselves hastily having to construct theological explanations to justify events which had already occurred. Again, fundamental questions about the nature of decision-making were raised, such as to what extent consensus should precede action and to what extent such actions might lead to a new consensus. Alternative models of authority were posited: on the one hand, those anxious not to disturb the prospects of reunion argued that such a momentous decision as ordaining women could only be taken by the whole of Christendom at some kind of universal conference, a 'Vatican III' in which Anglicans, Roman Catholics and the Orthodox could decide the issue together. On the other, those who believed that the ordination of women was the priority argued that the experiment should be tried in parts of Christendom – if it faded away, it would be seen to be contrary to God's will, but if it took hold, it would show other Christian Churches the right path. These crucial questions were, however, barely addressed, let alone resolved, by the bishops gathered at Canterbury. Instead, the fruit of their labours was a creaking, pragmatic compromise which had the undoubted virtue of keeping the worldwide Anglican Church afloat, but left it leaking below the waterline.

On the eve of the conference, both the Orthodox and Roman Catholic Churches added to Anglican discomfort by appealing to the bishops to desist from the ordination of women. Orthodox leaders, increasingly alarmed at what they saw as creeping Anglican liberalism, dug in their heels, making clear their view that such an innovation was 'absolutely inadmissible'. A slightly softer tone was adopted by Cardinal Hume, who said in a newspaper interview that it would be 'a pity' for any Church to act by itself on such a sensitive issue. But as the bishops took note of the warnings, they found themselves confronting turbulence much closer to home: as they took their seats in Canterbury cathedral for the conference's opening service, they can hardly have missed four women recently ordained in America or Canada seated sedately in the congregation, fully robed in clerical attire. Later, as part of a series of threats,

72

protests, demonstrations and prayers, women campaigners including Kroll staged a 24-hour prayer vigil outside Westminster Abbey. As the bishops arrived there for a special service half-way through the conference, they had to 'run the gauntlet' of the campaigners, who were performing symbolic street theatre outside.

When the issue of women priests was eventually debated openly by the conference, after private discussions among groups of bishops, the fragile unity obtained among the bishops on issues such as human rights, apartheid and the role of the bishops was strained. They had already voted to downgrade the importance of the Anglican Consultative Council, preferring instead to rely on meetings of the primates of the individual Anglican Churches to sort out future disputes. Then they were lectured by Canon John Macquarrie, Lady Margaret Professor of Divinity at Oxford and Anglicanism's foremost theologian, who said individual Churches should have deferred action until the Lambeth Conference, and vigorously rebuked the American Episcopal Church. Though in favour of women priests, he said the change should not be made until a 'substantial consensus' had been obtained. 'I do not think that 1,900-year-old tradition can be overturned by a simple majority vote at perhaps a single meeting of the governing body of one part of the Church,' he said. But he nevertheless dealt a severe blow to the opponents by suggesting that the maleness of the priesthood was a peripheral rather than essential part of Anglican tradition and belief. One of the main claims made by the proponents of women priests was that the issue was a secondary matter, a question of long-established practice and discipline (much as clerical celebacy is in the Roman Catholic Church) rather than a tenet of faith, and therefore something that could be introduced without altering the nature of the Church's fundamental doctrine. But the opponents held that the issue was a primary one, touching on core beliefs and therefore set in stone (a view shared by the Roman Catholic Church). This critical question was never satisfactorily resolved, though the English bishops would agree in a 1988 report that the distinction was, in this case, an irrelevancy because the issue of women priests was clearly linked with other questions which were undoubtedly primary, such as the nature of priesthood.

Unwilling or unable to force a showdown, the opponents engaged in a damage limitation exercise, spending long hours behind closed doors negotiating an acceptable compromise motion they could put their names to when it came to a vote in the final week of the conference. 'It was a typical Anglican thing,' remembers Leonard.

> We altered the phraseology of part of the motion from refer-ring to those who ordained women to those 'who had taken part in ordinations' who 'believe' they were valid. It did leave it to us to say they hadn't really been ordained or we didn't know. But a lot of us were appalled by Macquarrie's speech. He had always been against. I just felt at the time that it had been given away, and that we wouldn't recover from this.

After a relaxed debate, chaired by Coggan, the main motion was convincingly carried by 316 to 37 votes; the key areas of friction had been whittled away in tense sessions behind the scenes to permit the public show of unity. A proposal to impose a five-year moratorium on women's ordination threatened to reignite the debate, but it was defeated by two to one, despite some grumbles that the conference had brushed the most difficult issues under the carpet. But with Hong Kong, Canada, the United States and New Zealand already ordaining women (Australia and seven others were moving in that direction) there was never any serious prospect of a retreat on the central issue. The formula finally adopted – Resolution 21 – retro-spectively endorsed the actions of those autonomous Churches that had ordained women while simultaneously attempting to smooth Roman Catholic and Orthodox feelings. More significantly for internal unity, it said that those Churches which had ordained women and those which had not should remain 'in communion' (i.e. the state in which clergy ordained in any part of the worldwide Anglican Church should be recognized in all of it). In reality, this was a nonsense – Alice in Wonderland territory; women clergy were clearly far from universally acceptable. The somewhat dubious notion of 'impaired communion' would later be developed to describe the true situation. The conference left many critical issues unresolved. Nevertheless, it more than adequately fulfilled its primary function, that of sustaining the illusion that all was peace, light and brotherly love among the bishops.

The illusion was soon shattered, at least in the Church of England. Following the Lambeth Conference, the English bishops had judged that the time was right for a rerun of the women priests debate in the November meeting of the General Synod. Their motives were mixed; some who opposed women priests agreed to the debate in order to show how deep the divisions were. Supporters of female ordination thought that events abroad might influence the General Synod to swing back into line with its more progressive counterparts oversees. But, sadly for the would-be women priests waiting in the wings, it was a bad misjudgement; too few of the clergy had read the right script.

In the weeks before the November Synod meeting in Church House, there was a period of intense and often unedifying lobbying. The propaganda engines of both sides worked overtime to produce a profusion of pamphlets, open letters and arm twisting. The ultra traditionalist Anglo-Catholic group Ecclesia issued a declaration signed by 211 priests who said they would break communion with any bishop who ordained women. Meanwhile, nearly 1,000 lay people – from Peter Pears, the singer, and Derek Nimmo, the actor, to Sir John Burley, the former headmaster of Eton – signed a counter declaration in support of women's ordination. The contrast between conservative clergy and liberal laity was mirrored in the Synod; the motion to remove legal barriers was overwhelmingly carried by the bishops and the laity, but crushed by the clergy. As the result was announced to a packed Synod, a group of women in the public gallery, led by Kroll, shouted out: 'We asked for bread and you gave us a stone. Long live God.'

The debate was tense; one woman speaker was hissed when she accused opponents of women priests of 'being afraid of female sexuality'. It was also notable for the degree of organization displayed by the Anglo-Catholic group, which commanded the loyalty of about a third of the Synod's clergy. Members of the group were instructed to get into the chamber early so they could sit together and be able to catch the eye of the Synod chairman, who determined the order of speakers. They were also told to stay in their seats for the whole session, and to show no reaction to the speeches of the other side. During the debate it became increasingly clear that while many were sympathetic in principle to women priests, they could not stomach the consequences in practice. The then Bishop of London, Gerald Ellison, said that though he believed that women would one day be ordained, the atmosphere had become soured, the issue had polarized and Synod members had been bombarded by a mass of propaganda. 'I cannot think of anything that would be more disruptive of the peace of the Church than to pass this resolution by a small majority, do all the work that it requires, be subjected to propaganda one way or the other, build up hopes, only to defeat the whole project when we come to the special majorities which will ultimately be required,' he said. Despite a fervent appeal from Coggan – 'This is a deciding hour for the Church of England' – the clergy preferred the caution of Ellison. Coggan's particular disappointment was with the attitude of the Synod; he wrote to a friend: 'I sense a resurgence of party spirit of the kind that ever since I became a bishop in 1956 I have tried to avoid.'

If the 1975 debate had scarred the traditionalists, then the 1978 debate inflicted equivalent wounds on the pro-ordination camp. The sense of betrayal they felt was intense, and acted as a catalyst for the formation of the Movement for the Ordination of Women, a pressure group willing to ditch the gradualist approach adopted by its more genteel predecessor, the Anglican Group for the Ordination of Women. Established in July 1979, its executive included some powerful figures who were not always in harmony about the best way forward, and there was tension between the moderates and the radicals. Its most prominent supporters among the bishops included Stanley Booth-Clibborn at Manchester, Barry Rogerson at Bristol and Ronald Bowlby at Southwark. From its small London base, the movement – which was chaired on non-hierarchical lines by a 'moderator' – set up branches in every diocese and organized special services and 'witnessing' at ordinations, published alternative liturgies, pamphlets, and a magazine called *Chrysalis*, and produced T-shirts bearing slogans such as

'God is an equal opportunities employer, pity about the Church' and tea towels reading: 'A woman's place is in the House . . . of Bishops'. McClatchey, a founder member of MOW who was to become its moderator, recalls:

> We were furious with the bishops because in 1975, it had been agreed that they would bring the issue back again when they thought the time was appropriate. Three years elapsed and they had done absolutely nothing to educate public opinion. In 1978 we realized we had to combine all our resources and quite specifically start a campaign. We knew we had to galvanize public opinion if we were to move those clergy in Synod. Women had been a pain to the bishops for a long time; we made it very clear that we had no intention of giving up and being quiet.

6

The Wilderness
(1980–84)

Initially at least, the appointment of Robert Runcie to succeed
Coggan in 1979 was an occasion for rejoicing among opponents of
women priests. Though Runcie described himself as a 'radical
Catholic', his historian's sense of the continuity of Church tradition
and his profound respect for the position of the Orthodox Church
within it marked him out as an ally. He did little to dispel that
impression – his first words as Archbishop-elect on the issue were
that the arguments deployed against the ordination of women had
been 'insufficiently considered'. In truth, like his Anglo-Catholic
predecessor William Temple, he felt deep misgivings about the
intellectual credibility of the negative arguments, but he was
anxious that women priests should not derail the delicate understanding he was establishing with the Orthodox, a project in which
he had invested much personal capital. Given his own Anglo-
Catholic roots, he was also emotionally inclined to ultimate reunion
with Rome, an area in which dramatic advances still appeared likely.

But on this issue, as on others, Runcie was to shift his position
during his term of office. He became increasingly disillusioned with
the unity movement, while his belief that the Church of England
needed the vitality of women priests grew. For the first time, he also
saw things from an international perspective. As the nominal leader
of the whole Anglican Church, he began to perceive his primary
duty in terms of balancing the conflicting wishes of its constituent
parts, some of which already recognized women priests. Indeed, he
came to regard the preservation of internal unity as one of his highest

priorities; he did not relish going down in history as the Archbishop who presided over the disintegration of Anglicanism. As a result, he found himself holding the ring between warring parties, a role which fitted him temperamentally and philosophically but which enraged those of his critics who yearned for the smack of firm leadership, and who accused him of appearing to be all things to all people. In the memorable phrase coined by Frank Field, the Labour MP, Runcie nailed his colours to the fence. This impression was reinforced by an intellectual diffidence – despite possessing a subtle analytical mind, he was loath to commit his views to paper – and an over-sensitivity to the inherent weakness of his constitutional authority within the Church, which inhibited him from throwing his weight around. For him, however, compromise was never a craven word. He deployed his considerable personal charm to pursuade and cajole; diplomacy was preferred to diktat.

But the forces that Runcie was attempting to balance often seemed beyond his control. The American Church was increasingly in the sway of radicals, who were impatient to implement a liberal agenda which would put them even further out of kilter with the rest of the worldwide Church. Runcie had little real power to restrain them (though he did pursuade them to delay consecrating women bishops). Only later in his term of office did he begin to introduce a new idea of constitutional authority designed to shift the balance of power towards the centre and rein in the more destructive impulses of the individual churches. In the meantime, he appeared to his detractors to be drifting towards the liberal centre of gravity, like a swimmer sucked into a whirlpool. Inevitably, there was a backlash among the traditionalists. Any hopes they may have harboured that the former tank commander and holder of the Military Cross might do for the Church what Margaret Thatcher had done for the political landscape soon faded. Instead of leadership by conviction, they had leadership by committee and consensus. As their paranoia grew, they began to imagine that he had never harboured any sympathy for them, and that he was, in fact, at the centre of a sinister liberal conspiracy to oust them from the Church. But to impute such Machiavellian motives to Runcie was to misunderstand his principled pragmatism.

He was soon confronted with the issue of women priests. The question of what visiting rights the Church of England should extend to women lawfully ordained abroad was to be placed firmly back on the agenda by McClatchey in 1982, following the Synod's rejection in 1979 of initial attempts to lift the ban (a position he endorsed at that time). Before then, however, Runcie promoted another significant step for women; he was one of the two bishops who successfully moved in the November 1981 Synod that legislation should be drawn up to allow them to be ordained as full deacons. Although as deaconesses they had been able to fulfil all the duties open to a deacon (except the solemnization of marriage, where it is a legal requirement that it be performed by 'a clerk in holy orders') the order of deaconess had never been confirmed as 'holy' in the Church of England; members of it (there were at that stage 320 in the Church of England, over a third of whom wanted to become priests) were, technically, lay women. For the House of Bishops, it was a matter of correcting the anomaly. The 1978 Lambeth Conference had asked regional Churches which did not ordain women deacons to do so, in accordance with a resolution passed by the 1968 Lambeth Conference. The issue was to provide an arena for shadow boxing on the larger question of women priests. But it differed in one important respect; it split the ranks of the opponents of women priests between those who felt they could not oppose the ordination of women as deacons and those who feared the development was the thin end of the wedge.

Despite his backing for women deacons, Runcie was still perceived as a sceptic on women priests. In 1981, he aroused the wrath of both the women's movement and the diehard Protestants by becoming the first Archbishop in modern times to lead the 15,000-strong annual pilgrimage to the Anglo-Catholic shrine of Our Lady of Walsingham, Norfolk. He further infuriated the women's movement when he outlined his arguments against the ordination of women at an international meeting held in Sheffield and organized under the aegis of the World Council of Churches, which appeared to many to have adopted political correctness as an article of faith. To a distinctly chilly reception, Runcie said he was still 'listening and learning' to what the 'Spirit is saying to the

Churches' about the ordination of women. But he added that the women's movement was no longer simply feminist.

> It divides between those who want to burn their bras, refuse to marry and insist on doing all that men do – even to playing games which are anatomically painful – and those who seek for something more difficult to articulate. That something is the freedom to be women. I hope in the rhetoric of the feminist movement the Churches will not lose the real message of a Christian feminist movement which is about complementarity in ministry and the unity of the sexes in the Godhead.

But the pro-ordination lobby's disappointment over Runcie's lukewarm stance on women's ordination was as nothing compared to its dismay at the appointment of Graham Leonard to the key bishopric of London, third in order of precedence in the hierarchy. It was widely rumoured that Mrs Thatcher, an admirer of his, had appointed him to London over the head of the then Bishop of Durham, John Habgood, a leading liberal. In fact the two names had, unusually, been presented to Downing Street in no order of preference. Habgood, an intellectual whose aloofness earned him respect rather than affection, would later be handed the even bigger prize of York. Leonard, meanwhile, who as Bishop of Truro had been little more than a gadfly on the flanks of the Church's liberal establishment, found in London that he had a formidable power base from which to consolidate his position as leader of the traditionalist wing of the Church. Not only was the diocese a bastion of Anglo-Catholicism (every form could be found there, from the exotic to the antiquarian), but he could also cultivate his political friends. Thatcher and a number of Tory Cabinet Ministers were regular visitors to his Barton Street flat, a few hundred yards from the Houses of Parliament. In fact, he soon found that he had more affinity with them than many of his fellow bishops.

Over the next decade, he and Runcie were to have a pivotal relationship. Temperamentally they were very different. Whereas Runcie's crumpled features were often wracked with uncertainty, Leonard, pipe-smoking, deliberate, with a penchant for popish ecclesiastical outfits, could appear too assured, inflexible, even legalistic. In private, Runcie could be decisive, even waspish, and Leonard unexpectedly warm. Their formal relations were never more than cordial; philosophically, they were worlds apart. For Leonard, Runcie represented some of the worst aspects of Anglicanism, presiding over the House of Bishops as if it were an extension of the Athenaeum in which the worst solecism was to upset the other members. 'Robert was primarily motivated by the desire not to upset the club,' he says. 'He was a club man from his early days, and the attitude was that no one minded if you had odd views providing you did not press them to the point where you actually behaved as if they were true. It was considered bad manners.' Even more damning is his allegation that many of his colleagues in the House of Bishops were unwilling or unable to take theology seriously.

> When in the 1960s, you had the influence of extreme liberalism, there was no real appeal to theology, and as a result it was thought we must not rock the boat. Liberals have got away with rocking the boat, but they ran the club. The House of Bishops adopted an essentially pragmatic approach to issues. This has always disturbed me, and it is what I call the theological levity of the House of Bishops.

Runcie is scathing about Leonard's charges.

> It is very easy to make that sort of allegation when you find yourself in a minority and unable to argue the majority out of their firmly held convictions. There is little doubt that Graham got a hearing, but did not carry the House. This was sometimes coupled with a sense that he had been confronted with the choice of whether he was going to lead the Catholic movement in the Church of England or be Bishop of London, and he seemed to be representing a constituency beyond London. That sort of distinction between London, which became ministerially very much the headquarters of a club, and the rest of the House of Bishops did show itself in debates.

But it would be very hard to think of one of the strongest proponents of the ordination of women, like John Baker, Bishop of Salisbury, lacking any passion compared to the Bishop of London. You wouldn't easily charge him with theological levity. And when they argued the case, I think the bishops tended to be convinced by the arguments he advanced. When it came to serious debate, there were a limited number of articulate participants in the House of Bishops but the bishops in general were capable of forming a mind. It is part of the business of the bishops to have collegiality, and the very word collegiality has the smell of a club.

If Leonard was to find himself increasingly at odds with his episcopal colleagues, his first task was to stamp his authority on his own diocese; within a few months of his arrival, a woman priest ordained in the United States had illegally celebrated Communion in the heart of London, in the deanery of St Paul's cathedral. The incident not only reinforced how the tensions created by women being ordained abroad was reaching snapping point, but also brought Leonard into direct conflict for the first time with the bishop who was to become his long-time adversary, the arch-liberal John Spong, of Newark, New Jersey, on America's east coast. Their often torrid exchanges over the years exemplified the fundamental divide between conservatives and progressives.

Leonard had visited the Episcopal Church in America a number of times in the 1970s, and felt it was becoming increasingly secularized. At the 1978 Lambeth Conference, he had seen how they exercised an influence far outweighing the size of their constituency. He was increasingly aware of the pressures it would exert on the Church of England. So when Elizabeth Canham, an English deaconess controversially ordained as a priest by Spong in America, returned to celebrate Communion in London, he saw it as 'aimed at myself' and 'part of the pressure to push things along'. Canham, a former divinity teacher, at whose ordination service in December 1981 the former Bishop of Southwark, Mervyn Stockwood, had preached, had been invited to celebrate by the Dean of St Paul's, Alan Webster. Members of MOW, of which the Dean's wife

Margaret was a leading light, felt that the ecclesiastical law was ambiguous; while it clearly barred women priests from celebrating publicly, it was not so clear about private ceremonies. Leonard, however, was in no doubt; no one from outside the Church of England was allowed to perform an ecclesiastical function in England, publicly or privately, without the prior permission of the Archbishop of Canterbury and the bishop of the diocese concerned. He asked Runcie to dissuade clergy from allowing such services and gained broad support for his interpretation of the law, including from, among others, Stockwood. Runcie issued a mild rebuke. But the incident was not to deter MOW, which issued a defiant statement declaring its support for 'women priests who break bread privately in this country.' Amid increasing polarization between the two sides, the situation was further inflamed when, at a MOW conference in Derbyshire in April 1982, two diocesan bishops – Stanley Booth Clibborn of Manchester and Cyril Bowles of Derby – received Holy Communion (in an inter-denominational chapel) at the hands of a woman ordained a priest in New Zealand. It was obvious to all that feminist dissent would continue to grow rather than diminish.

Meanwhile, the Anglo–Catholic cause received a major fillip with the visit of Pope John Paul II to Britain in May 1982, at the climax of which the Pope and Runcie knelt together in silent prayer in Canterbury cathedral. It was a potent symbol. John Paul II may hardly have heard of the Anglican Church when he became Pope four years earlier, but his wish to see England gathered back into the Catholic fold like an errant sheep was transparent. The Pope's tour – which included a trip to Liverpool where he was heckled by Paisleyite Protestants – represented the zenith of Anglo–Catholic hopes that reunion was achievable within their lifetimes. The euphoria was tangible. George Austin, who has always been more Anglo than Catholic, recalls that 'for the first time we really thought we were breaking down the barriers.' For Peter Geldard, the occasion had a particular poignancy.

> In 1981, it was suggested that we should give the Pope, as a sign of unity, a red stole which had on it the arms of Canterbury, the Papal arms and the dove of the Holy Spirit. I

took it with me on a pilgrimage to Lourdes, the Catholic shrine in France, but the Pope could not be there as he had been shot by a would-be assassin. So I gave it to Cardinal Gantin who took it to the Pope's bedside in Rome and gave it to him. I thought that was the end of it. Imagine my joy when, on the television monitor in the cathedral on the day, I saw him coming around the corner and he was wearing the stole I had given him. That was a high moment. One read so much into the words he said – the successor of St Gregory meets the successor of St Augustine. There was a sense with Runcie that this was a high point for him too.

But the impetus was short lived. Hopes among liberal Anglicans that the Vatican might prove flexible on the issue of women priests evaporated; indeed, the Pope was more conservative on this issue than his predecessors. By the mid-1980s, there was little evidence that real progress was being made towards corporate reunion, and Runcie encountered growing difficulty persuading his colleagues to hold back on women priests to prevent upsetting the process. While Anglican and Roman Catholic theologians were discovering that vast areas of agreement existed between their Churches, and Runcie expressed his willingness to see the Pope as a 'universal primate' or nominal head of a united Christendom – Rome showed little enthusiasm for the project. Increasingly frustrated, the Anglo-Catholics felt that if Rome could make some positive move, such as the recognition of Anglican orders, it would revive the reunion project and stop the ordination of women campaign dead in its tracks. Geldard recalls that Canon Gareth Bennett, the Oxford don who was later to pen the anonymous attack on Runcie in the Crockford's preface, went to see the Archbishop in the mid-1980s to try to persuade him to nail his colours to the unity mast.

Garry basically told him, you can either back the ordination of women, which will result in an easy life, or you can commit yourself to reunion, which is a harder ride but which would make you the best Archbishop since the Reformation. Runcie was trying to ride two horses like a circus act, keeping a foot on each. In the end he had to decide which one was going. He may have got signals from Rome, rightly or wrongly, that one was slowing down, and all his backing would not make it go forward. So in order to keep on a horse at all, he decided to back the ordination of women.

Increasingly, however, Runcie's primary concern was internal rather than external unity; within Anglicanism rather than with the Roman Catholic and Orthodox Churches. The July 1982 Synod was dominated by the issue of women priests, in the form of two motions. The first, which required a two-thirds majority, set out the terms for a covenant of unity with the Methodist and United Reform Churches, an attempt to revive the ill-fated Anglican/ Methodist scheme of the 1970s. If adopted, there would have been a mutual recognition of ministries and an acceptance that women ordained as ministers in the Free Churches were priests in the eyes of the Church of England. It was on this issue that the whole project stumbled; it was defeated by the House of Clergy. The leading role of the Anglo-Catholics in its demise would not easily be forgiven.

The second motion, tabled by Diana McClatchey, asked that women priests ordained overseas who visited Britain should be allowed to exercise their ministry during their stay. It called for legislation to be drawn up to give diocesan bishops the power to permit a woman priest to celebrate Communion in an English parish church, just as a visiting male priest could do. To the advocates of women priests, it was a matter of justice and of regularizing the 'underground' services which were being conducted by visiting American priests with increasing regularity. But to the opponents, such legislation would have conceded the principle that women could validly celebrate Holy Communion before the Church of England had formally made such a decision. Despite the defeat of the covenanting plan the previous day, and his previous opposition to anything likely to complicate relations with the Orthodox, Runcie threw his weight behind the motion. He was aware of the growing anger among bishops in New Zealand, Canada and America that the women they were ordaining could not officiate in England. He told the Synod that, for the sake of the 'coherence' of the worldwide Anglican Church, some movement was needed; his intervention won the day, and the process of drawing up legislation to effect the change was begun. But Runcie's instinct to delay the final decision on any contentious issue in the hope that consensus would develop in the intervening period was soon in evidence. To the anger of the women's ordination lobby, when the draft measure came back to the Synod, Runcie, Habgood and senior officials took the decision that it was of such a sensitive nature that it should be voted on by all the diocesan synods (a lengthy process) before it could return to the General Synod, where it would require a two-thirds majority to succeed. It would not reach its 'final approval' stage until 1986.

Meanwhile, in an atmosphere of uneasy calm, the militants within the pro-women movement kept up their programme of direct action. For some, who regularly experienced the patronizing slights of unthinking male colleagues, the dictum 'don't get angry, get even' was too passive. In July 1980, a group were frogmarched out of St Paul's cathedral in London when they held up banners during an ordination ceremony protesting at the exclusion of women. In the summer of 1983, about 100 MOW supporters staged a 'rebel service' outside Southwark cathedral during an ordination ceremony. Reciting a 'wilderness liturgy' to reflect their belief that they had been cast out by the Church, the deaconesses involved complained that they had wanted to be presented to the bishop alongside the men being ordained that day, but their protest met with strong opposition. Some churchmen had threatened to give them a slow handclap. Inside, Ronald Bowlby, Bishop of Southwark, who as the MOW's vice-moderator was committed to the ordination of women, nevertheless condemned the demonstration for ruining the day for those involved in the official ceremony. The mixed reactions to the protest highlighted the growing divisions within the pro-women lobby over tactics, between those who believed the time had come for militancy and those who feared an over-aggressive approach would be counter-productive. This inherent tension would later lead to splits in the movement.

Far away from these high-profile events, however, women were gradually gaining ground in key areas of the Church. The number of deaconesses had risen sharply, and they were of a higher calibre. Many of them were married women and so needed little or no pay. In 1969 there had been 81 deaconesses; by 1984, there were 312. At the same time the number of men wanting to become priests was declining. Women were also taking on positions of greater responsibility. Though they could not consecrate the bread and wine, pronounce absolution or conduct weddings, a growing number were effectively running parishes. Others were university or hospital chaplains. The increasing visibility and obvious proficiency of these women ministers worked to break down prejudice against them. The mood in society at large was more confused, however. Though the Sex Discrimination Act was improving women's employment prospects, there was the beginnings of a backlash against the more extreme elements of the 'Women's Lib' movement, personified by the women of the Greenham Common peace camp. The economic recession and political atmosphere had also led to calls for women to return to their traditional role in the kitchen. Although the majority of women working in the Church were middle class and middle-of-the-road, the more strident, feminist image of some of the prominent campaigners on the issue often deterred even their own more tentative supporters. While surveys showed that over 80 per cent of the general public were in favour of women priests, a much more accurate snapshot of the mind of the Church was provided by the figures for weekly churchgoers: while two-thirds of them were in favour, a third were adamantly against.

At the same time, with hope for reunion with Rome at an all time high, the Anglo-Catholics were experiencing something of a revival. Two special conferences at Loughborough in 1979 and 1983 were attended by thousands, the vast majority of whom affirmed their staunch opposition to women priests. The numbers of liberal Anglo-Catholics who supported women priests and who resented being tarred with the traditionalist brush were still small; they were not to form their own Affirming Catholicism group until the late 1980s. The resurgence of mainstream Anglo-Catholicism, however, owed much to a widespread reaction against the climate of liberalism within the Church; the Anglo-Catholics seemed to stand for something more permanent and uncompromising than the 'spirit of the age', which many of them claimed persuasively was the true impetus behind the liberals' misguided efforts to elevate women to the priesthood. In 1983, the Anglo-Catholics also celebrated the 150th anniversary of the start of their movement, the celebrated sermon preached by John Keble in Oxford in which he reclaimed the Church of England's Catholic tradition. Runcie, though regarding himself as coming from a broader Catholic tradition than that encompassed by the Anglo-Catholics, nevertheless told the movement in a sermon in Oxford to mark the anniversary: 'We are meant to praise a movement that goes on, not to bury it. Be hopeful. Be loyal to your Church.' Within two years, however, one of his closest friends and mentors, Peter Cornwell, was to follow Newman to Rome. Cornwell, who had been vice-principal of Cuddesdon theological college when Runcie was principal in the 1960s, was tipped for high Anglican office and was rector of the historic University Church of St Mary the Virgin in Oxford. So when he announced in a sermon to his congregation that he was resigning to join the Roman Catholic Church, it sent a *frisson* through the Church of England. Though his departure had not been specifically triggered by the issue of women priests, it was powerfully symbolic: Newman – whose own conversion to Rome had scandalized the Victorians – had been vicar of the church and Keble had used its pulpit to deliver his Assize sermon. Oxford, a bastion of Anglo-Catholicism, was awash with rumours for months that other senior clergy or college deans would follow, triggering the largest exodus since Newman. Several other Anglican priests did follow Cornwell, but there was no exodus.

By November 1984, it had been six years since the General Synod had so dramatically thrown out the proposal that the time was right to introduce legislation to ordain women priests. Much had changed since then; the activists in the women's movement had stepped up their pressure through direct action and, more importantly, MOW had been engaged in a national education campaign to win over hearts and minds in the pews, a campaign aided by the example of the growing number of women deaconesses active in the parishes. But not all the signs were propitious. Abroad, the experiences of the American Episcopal Church, which had been seriously split on the issue, were salutory. Since the Minneapolis Convention in 1976, 38 dioceses had declined to ordain women. In the Anglican Church worldwide, although more than 600 women had been ordained priests, the momentum was also faltering; the vast majority of provinces had not yet followed the lead of the United States, Canada and New Zealand. There were also grave doubts at the heart of the Church of England's leadership about the timing of any further moves towards women priests, and the havoc it might wreak on the burgeoning ecumenical movement. So it was not the House of Bishops which brought the issue back but just one of their number, the former MOW moderator and old Etonian liberal Ronald Bowlby. MOW demonstrated its new organizational talents by mobilizing its support among the bishops and clergy; in the run up to the debate, a group of 15 of the former, including Booth Clibborn, signed a letter to *The Times* and 1,000 clergy put their names to a petition calling for the ordination of women. But there was still a widespread expectation that the motion would fail.

During the debate, traditionalists issued dire warnings of the consequences of going down the route of women priests, saying the Church would tear itself apart. Gareth Bennett, the traditionalists' in-house theologian, told the Synod that while there could be change within a tradition the problem was 'to distinguish between true development from what is merely contemporary fashion'. Runcie was in a dilemma. He confessed to the Synod that he believed the arguments in favour of admitting women 'tipped the balance favourably', but he nevertheless urged caution. He conceded he had consistently 'driven down the middle of the road' on the issue. 'To grow towards the ordination of women, we must first take steps towards a wider experience of women's ministry,' he said. Unity talks with other Churches also had to be taken into account. 'I cannot conceal my conviction that we have a duty not to be seen to be acting in an abrasive and unfraternal disregard of very large Catholic bodies with whom we share the very fundamentals of the faith.' But the Synod was more in tune with the note struck by Archbishop Habgood of York who said that, while sharing many of Runcie's doubts about rushing into such a major step, 'to defeat it at this stage would be a crushing blow for a cause in which I believe.'

Many feared that, by ordaining women, the Church of England would be cutting itself off from the Christian mainstream and setting itself up as some funny little independent entity, he said. But by adopting synodical government it had already gravely complicated its relations with the Roman Catholic and Orthodox Churches. Crucially, Graham Leonard – who would have provided the heavyweight theological opposition – missed the debate through illness. Their defences weakened, the Anglo-Catholics concentrated their fire on practical implications of ordaining women. It was little match for the passion and principle of the proponents, who swept all before them. Runcie's cautions went unheeded and Bowlby's motion was carried in all three Houses by a total of 307 votes to 183, reversing the defeat of 1978. The size of the majority provoked astonishment, although the opponents took some comfort from the fact that a two-thirds majority would be required at the final approval stage of the legislation. Somewhat to its own surprise, therefore, the Church of England had embarked on the long and painful process of drawing up legislation designed to turn dreams into reality for the women's movement and into nightmares for the traditionalists. The ensuing dissension would divide a generation.

7

Deus Ex Machina

(1985–86)

With relatively little fanfare, the Synod gave final approval the following summer for legislation to allow women to be ordained deacons. The matter had been so overshadowed by the larger issue of women priests that its significance was largely overlooked. For the first time, women were to be admitted to the previously male-only preserve of holy orders and titled 'Reverend'; bar consecrating the bread and wine at Communion and pronouncing absolution, they would be able to do anything a male priest could do. For all practical purposes, they were a scintilla away from the priesthood. Nevertheless, what seemed to be symbolically and pragmatically a major advance for the cause of women priests had met with surprisingly little resistance from the majority of Anglo–Catholics, who could have hampered the reform if they had united against it. But opponents of women priests such as Leonard – who was himself to ordain women deacons the following year after the legislation had passed through its Parliamentary hoops – felt they could not mount sustainable intellectual or theological challenge to the development. While aware of the force of the 'thin end of the wedge' argument, they accepted the evidence of biblical scholarship that women deacons had existed in the early Church. Since one of the most powerful objections to women priests relied on the conclusions of the same scholarship that women had not been ordained to the priesthood at that time, they could hardly reject women deacons and claim to be consistent. Some of them also believed that the admission of women to the bottom rung of holy orders would make little impact on the women priest debate; the two issues, they felt, were clearly distinct because women deacons were not called on to represent Christ at Communion. The most optimistic, or naive, of them hoped that a distinctive and permanent diaconate would evolve (though several attempts to introduce this into the legislation – by Gareth Bennett among others – proved unsuccessful). The order was treated as an apprenticeship for the priesthood, but why, some reasoned, should it not become an end in itself, a limited ministry with which women could be content?

Not all were so sanguine. A rump of hardline Anglo-Catholics refused to believe that women would be content to remain deacons for the rest of their lives and forgo the greater prize of priesthood. Instead, they rightly feared that the arrival in shires and inner cities of this new breed of fully-fledged clergywomen, whose responsibilities were barely distinguishable from those of a priest, would only advance MOW's efforts to familiarize churchgoers with the unfamiliar concept of women at the altar. And what of reunion with Rome and the Orthodox, neither of whom countenanced altar girls, let alone women deacons? The disagreement caused a deep and painful rift within the ranks of the traditionalists and fatally split any resistance to the legislation permitting women deacons.

'There was no doubt that women were admitted to the diaconate in primitive times,' says Leonard. 'That being so I could not honestly oppose it. I knew I would be misunderstood, but nevertheless I knew that if I refused to do this I would also be misunderstood and accused of being purely a misogynist. I still think I was right.' Geldard represents the hardline view. 'I think Graham believed you could live in a pure world where you could separate the scholarly, academic solution from the pragmatic political solution,' he counters. 'The pragmatic consequence was that once women were deacons you could not stop the pressure. They would be seen alongside male deacons, but when male deacons went forward to the priesthood, they would not. They also exploited the fact that they could take all the service bar four paragraphs. Plus they had a presence in the Synod's House of Clergy which affected the voting.' In retrospect, many opponents of women priests concede that they might have underestimated the significance of women deacons. At the time, however, they had other things on their mind.

Like Parliament, the Synod membership is re-elected every five years, and the elections that took place in the autumn of 1985 were inevitably dominated by the issue of women priests. The number of candidates wanting to join this often stultifying democratic forum reached record levels - every Synod seat was contested by an average of three people. Even John Gummer, one of the most artic-ulate Anglo-Catholics, who had just been deposed as Tory party chairman, had to fight for his Synod seat in an election which rapidly assumed many of the unseemly trappings of its secular counterpart. MOW (3,600-strong by them) organized a slick campaign from its tiny London headquarters. While not adopting an official 'slate' of approved candidates, it made clear in publicity material which of them enjoyed its blessing. In one of its main campaign themes, it stressed the Church's waste of talent, arguing that while the number of men coming forward for ordination was declining sharply, 300 able women were waiting in the wings.

Despite its own often abrasive election tactics, the movement was not adverse to deploring the 'unsavoury' political manoeuvrings of its opponents who, alarmed at the professionalism of MOW, had formed a new organization which brought together for the first time members of the conservative Evangelical and Anglo-Catholic wings of the Church, an unlikely alliance of the Low Church and High Church. Cumbersomely titled the Association for the Apostolic Ministry, its main aim was to fight women priests, but it also shared a common enemy in the hydra of liberalism. Its supporters ranged from heavyweight Evangelical theologians such as Roger Beckwith of Latimer House, Oxford, to Anglo-Catholic bishops like Kemp and Richard Rutt of Leicester. The new organization was widely seen as a breakaway church-in-waiting, hanging the threat of schism over the head of the Church of England like a sword of Damocles. Like any deterrent, however, its efficacy depended in large part on whether the other side was convinced that the threat could or would ever be carried out. Many of the most fervent supporters of women priests, who anyway had difficulty believing that their opponents were driven by anything more profound than misogyny, were dubious. 'I thought there was a great element of blackmail and bluff about it,' says Diana McClatchey.

> I had to learn by experience how deeply they felt. We believed
> that their fears would be dispelled as they saw women clergy
> in practice, as deaconesses and then deacons. But I remember
> being contradicted by a nun after I had made a rather belit-
> tling comment. She said she knew how deep their pain went
> and that it was not going to disappear.

Leading Anglo-Catholics were to expend much of their energy over
the next few years trying to convince the wobbling middle-of-the-
road church membership that their threat was no bluff. It was a
strategy fraught with peril because it implicitly recognized that
women might, one day, be ordained as priests. Some anti-ordination campaigners felt this line weakened their arguments against the
principle of ordaining women. Leonard kept his options open:
while disclaiming suggestions that he might lead a future breakaway
Church, he nevertheless attended a meeting of 100 priests in
Oxford specifically to discuss the practicalities of establishing a
parallel institution for traditionalists alongside the official one.
Such a 'continuing Church of England' would, its supporters
claimed, merely be the legitimate continuation of the present institution of that name; it would be the bulk of the Church which, by
ordaining women, would be drifting away, like a ship that breaks
anchor. As a result, such a continuing Church could, they believed,
legitimately make a claim for a share of Church funds and property.

The notion of a parallel Church – a legally watertight entity
which could coexist with the main body of the Church of England
but which was entirely discreet, with its own hierarchy, administra-
tion, parishes and theological colleges – was very attractive to many
traditionalists. Such an organization could, they believed, be established in a number of ways, as a series of 'non-geographical'
dioceses which could take under their wing the traditionalist
parishes scattered around the country; as a 'third province' alongside the two existing provinces of Canterbury and York; or as an
international network, linking up traditionalists from Papua New
Guinea to Texas. For many traditionalists, some form of parallel

Church was the bottom line if women were ordained, and they were determined to ensure that any legislation contained at least elements of it on which they could build. But such a parallel Church was heresy to most of the bishops; it was an open wound, schism made flesh.

As if the atmosphere was not febrile enough, the Americans then tossed in a hand grenade. The Episcopal Church - already split over the issue of women priests and losing members - had just elected an arch-liberal, Edward Browning, as its presiding bishop. In September, its bishops went one further; they voted overwhelmingly to appoint a woman to their ranks. Though they also agreed not to go ahead before consulting other Anglican Church leaders, a number of the American bishops wanted immediate action. Spong provocatively declared his intention to appoint a woman as a suffragan (assistant) bishop in his Newark diocese as soon as possible. 'As the moment draws nearer when episcopacy will open to women, opponents are beginning to recycle all the arguments of the past and make dire threats of chaos and schism,' he wrote in his diocesan newsletter. 'The Bishop of London, Graham Leonard, thinks so little of the Church decision-making processes that he threatens to encourage the division of the Church of England into two separate bodies if his point of view opposing women is not sustained.' Spong continued: 'The discredited biblical argument continues to be heard from no less a person than Pope John Paul II.' Though Spong was on the extreme liberal wing of the American Church, the American decision, typically, took little account of sensitivities overseas. The general expectation had been that no women would be elevated to the episcopate until at least 1988, when the Lambeth Conference could set a general policy. Leonard indignantly described the prospect of women bishops as 'the final straw', saying it was difficult enough to live in a worldwide Anglican Church with women priests, but women bishops would render it impossible. His misgivings were echoed by others, both in England and in other parts of the Anglican world. Bishops are supposed to be focuses of unity, they argued, but a woman bishop would be a focus of disunity. A large number of traditionalist bishops, not to mention clergy and laity, would not accept that she could operate as a priest, let alone as a bishop; not only would they doubt her ability to consecrate bread and wine, but they would regard any ordinations she might perform as invalid and a farce. Even the men she ordained would not be valid priests. The very structure of Anglicanism, in both functional and theological terms, was built on the mutual recognition of ministries. If bishops could not 'do business' with each other – if, in theological terminology, they were 'out of communion' with one another – the worldwide Church would be in danger of fragmenting. Lambeth Conferences could become a nightmare, boycotted by dozens of bishops (Leonard was one who said he might not be able to attend). The Church would also be broken at a more profound level; it could no longer fulfil one of its core spiritual purposes, that of representing to the world an image of a united community of believers. Potentially, it was the gravest crisis Runcie faced; he would require all his powers of persuasion to avert a meltdown.

While the events in America had an impact on the Church of England, of more direct significance to the Synod elections was the 'Durham' factor. Even before his appointment as Bishop of Durham, David Jenkins, whose academic meanderings were more at home in a theology essay than on national television, had thoroughly unsettled the Church with his unorthodox (for a bishop) pronouncements on the resurrection and the Virgin birth. Two days after his consecration in York Minster, the ancient cathedral had been struck by lightning and seriously damaged in the ensuing fire, a sign, his detractors gleefully proclaimed, of divine displeasure. Jenkins was immediately accorded a special place in the demonology of the traditionalists, and his uncompromisingly provocative stance triggered a backlash which set back the liberal advance. Though more women were elected to the Synod then ever before, the liberals lost ground. The Evangelicals, Jenkins's fiercest critics, were rewarded with a better-than-ever representation in the Synod. In terms of the women priests debate, the shift in the balance of power was subtle. While supporters of female ordination had consolidated and even enlarged their majority in the House of Laity, the House of Clergy remained their Achilles' heel. There they were still short of the two-thirds majority they would need to ensure that the legislation cleared its final hurdle. They suffered a further set-back when the clergy voted for two prominent Anglo-Catholic opponents of women priests, David Silk, Archdeacon of Leicester, and Canon Peter Boulton, to the roles of Prolocutor (or spokesman) of the Lower Houses of the two Convocations of Canterbury and York. The Synod's Standing Committee, which derives its influence from setting the Synod's agenda, also lurched to the theological 'right', with the election to it of George Austin and Gareth Bennett.

The pro-women lobby's consolation prize was the election of David McClean, Professor of Law at Sheffield university, as chairman of the House of Laity, replacing Oswald Clark, one of the Anglo-Catholics' most skilled operators. McClean, a powerful advocate of women priests, was to play a key role in the unfolding saga, having been appointed by the Archbishops to prepare a blueprint for legislation to ordain women priests. In a typically Anglican way, the membership of the working party he chaired, whose task it was to draw up the range of options, deliberately reflected the broad spectrum of views on women priests, from the liberal to the traditional, and contained no built-in majority favouring the legislation. It was not a happy compromise. The ferocity of the debate to come was graphically illustrated by Leonard. On the eve of the newly-elected Synod's first meeting in Church House in November, he portrayed the Church of England as 'two express trains rushing towards each other on the same track'. If women were ordained, he warned, the Church would split irretrievably. An atmosphere of crisis pervaded the proceedings, and even the Queen appealed for unity when, as the Church of England's Supreme Governor, she officially opened the new Synod. But a chasm was opening up.

Runcie, as always, was attempting to keep a foot on both sides of the divide. His facility for damage limitation, for taking the heat out of the situation, would become increasingly evident in the coming months as the Church lurched from crisis to crisis. In March 1986, almost unnoticed in England, he successfully brokered a truce on the issue of women bishops. At a meeting of Anglican primates in Toronto, he persuaded his 28 fellow Church leaders to postpone any recommendation on whether the American Episcopalians should be permitted to consecrate the first woman bishop until the issue had been further examined. A committee was set up under the chairmanship of Archbishop John Grindrod, Primate of Australia. Runcie, meanwhile, strengthened his standing with the moderates by launching a powerful attack on both extremes, the conservatives who threatened to 'fossilize' the Church and 'righteous' radicals intolerant of other views. Once more he had won valuable breathing space and enhanced his reputation for ecclesiastical escapology.

His balancing act was again tested the following month when MOW organized a three-day celebration of women's ministry in Canterbury cathedral, attended by 40 overseas women priests and 2,500 supporters. Many hoped, indeed expected, that Runcie would preside at the service. The organizers were careful to ensure that the service was not highjacked by American activists who wanted to turn it into a political rally. But Runcie hesitated and eventually pulled out. McClatchey recalls: 'Initially he wanted to identify with it, but then it was pointed out to him by his advisers that if he identified with something MOW had organized, he really could not maintain his stance of impartiality.' Publicly, he decided to keep his distance, though privately he telephoned the organizers to congratulate them. In the event, the cathedral was so packed that a number of the bishops – who included 16 from Britain – had to give up their seats and sit on the floor. At the moment of consecration (conducted by a male priest), all the women priests in the pews raised their hands in prayer. It was a powerful moment which convinced many there, including McClatchey, that the momentum was unstoppable.

Meanwhile, however, the opponents of women priests had been mounting a counter-attack designed to persuade the Church that the cost of ordaining women was too high – that there would be too much blood on the carpet and too many shattered lives to justify what was at best a dubious departure from tradition. To counter the potency of the pro-ordination camp's argument that male chauvinism and misogyny rather then theology were the real motives of the opponents of women priests, the traditionalists founded Women Against the Ordination of Women, led by the formidable Synod veteran Dr Margaret Hewitt, a reader in sociology at Exeter university, who was distinguished by her booming voice and grand hats. This organization, composed entirely of women, was eventually to outstrip MOW in terms of numbers if not in influence. Much of the resistance to women at the altar had always derived from women in the pews; Dr Hewitt's handbagging style helped to undermine the feminists' refrain that these women's conservatism was the result of brutal oppression by men. Her no-nonsense view was that God had intended the Church to be patriarchial, like it or lump it. Meanwhile, the traditionalist members of the McClean committee were determined to upset the pro-ordination bandwaggon by demonstrating how divisive legislation to ordain women would be in practice. As a result the committee's final report, published in June 1986, contained a number of options which were, as the traditionalists had calculated they would be, anathema to the bishops and the majority of the Synod. McClatchey, who sat on the committee, said she had been so appalled by the tactics of some fellow members that she had been tempted to walk out. But because the purpose of the report had always been to put before the Synod a range of options, however extreme, she could do little. Therefore, though the committee's report may have declared a unanimous desire to preserve Church unity, in fact it read like a recipe for the apocalypse.

The most drastic option – put forward by Canon Brian Brindley of Oxford – envisaged splitting the Church into two official parts, one containing women priests and one not. Each parish and clergyman would be required to decide to which they belonged. Each would be autonomous and with their own bishops, property would have to be divided and at least one of them would have to be disestablished. Though not an entirely novel suggestion – Leonard, among others, had mooted the possibility of parallel Churches – it was the first time the prospect of a formal schism had been raised in an official report and it send tremors throughout the Church. It conjured up a chilling vision of rival dioceses, competing churches, embattled parishes, a burgeoning bureaucracy and deepening chaos as ordinary churchgoers were forced to check where they could receive Communion every time they travelled. The fabric of Anglicanism would be rent in two. Even the less frightening options in the report sounded outlandish (though some of them would eventually be incorporated into the legislation). They included: allowing parishes to have a veto over women priests; ensuring that diocesan bishops who did ordain women allowed an assistant bishop who did not to look after anti-women clergy and parishes; allowing 'anti' parishes to opt out of their own dioceses and come under the care of 'anti' bishops; and paying large sums in compensation to priests who resigned over the issue. MOW decried the report as 'scare tactics', claiming the committee was not representative of opinion in the Church as a whole. But the traditionalists felt they had scored a psychological victory by exposing the horrors that lay ahead if the Church went down the route of ordaining women priests. They took further comfort from a register compiled by Leonard of bishops, clergy and laity who regarded the ordination of women as 'imperilling the doctrine of the Church of England'. A few weeks before the crucial July Synod, it had been signed by 2,393 clergy (about 20 per cent of the total) and 12,466 laity, more than 7,500 of them women. However exaggerated the advocates of women priests claimed such propaganda to be, more and more ordinary members of the Church feared for its future.

The traditionalists were further bolstered by a remarkably frank exchange of letters between Runcie and the Vatican which had begun two years previously but was only published now by Lambeth Palace, two days before the York debates. The letters represented a theological dialogue of sorts, with Runcie attempting to persuade the Vatican that the ordination of women was not only permissible within the Christian tradition shared by both Churches but imperative. But both the Pope and Cardinal Willebrands, the President of the Secretariat for Promoting Christian Unity, made clear in separate letters that Rome could not countenance such a development. Once again, the Pope's letter seemed to suggest that he was primarily interested in preserving the purity of the Church of England - the rest of the Anglican Church was of less interest. Runcie's letters were also revealing, displaying his evident discomfort that his theological arguments in favour of ordaining women cut no ice in Rome. 'I am not myself convinced that action should be taken on ordination to the presbyterate by Anglicans alone, no matter how convincing the positive arguments, until there is a wider consensus in our Churches,' he wrote to Willebrands. If the priesthood was to be representative of humanity, he argued, it would be positively undermined if it remained a male-only preserve when society at large had rejected an exclusively male leadership. In a crushing reply, however, Willebrands told Runcie that he was simply wrong to think that the priesthood represented the whole of humanity. Priests represent Christ at the head of the body of the Church 'and we can never ignore the fact that Christ is a man,' wrote Willebrands, concluding: 'I wish simply to make the point that the arguments you relay cannot count as reasons for the radical innovation of ordaining women to the priesthood. The arguments do not negotiate the manifold theological issues which this matter raises.' In the eyes of Rome, therefore, the ordination of women was not only inexpedient but also contrary to the ordinance of God. The only crumb of comfort for Runcie was that the exchange of letters represented a public debate between Canterbury and Rome, something unthinkable fifty years before.

The Synod - more than half of whose members had only just been blooded - met at York university in July with two potentially explosive issues before it: the question of whether women ordained abroad could conduct services in the Church of England (thus regularizing the illegal services already taking place) and the McClean report. The atmosphere was more akin to a political than an ecclesiastical conference; groups huddled in corridors to plan tactics and lobbyists staged impromptu late night briefings in the campus bars. Both sides dropped dark hints of schism or defiance if the votes went against them. As often in the Church of England, much of the venom was whispered off-stage.

In the context of the larger question, the issue of whether a few hundred women priests ordained overseas should have the right, in specified circumstances and for a limited period, to preside at Communion services in this country might have seemed like a side-show, but the participants knew it was crucial. The proponents argued forcefully that justice demanded that women lawfully ordained abroad should have the same visiting rights as male overseas priests, and that such courtesies should be extended for the good of international Anglican relations. But the recently formed alliance of Anglo-Catholics and conservative Evangelicals had two aces up its sleeve. First, after intensive lobbing, the Archbishops had decided that the Women Ordained Abroad measure was so sensitive that it would require a two-thirds majority in each of the three Houses to succeed. Secondly, the Synod's Standing Committee decided to hold the debate on the measure on the opening Saturday of the Synod, three days before the McClean report was due to be discussed, a factor the opponents were quick to exploit. To accept the measure would, they contended, be putting the cart before the horse by pre-empting the substantive question of whether women should be allowed to be priests at all. Since they did not accept that a woman could validly celebrate Communion at all, the idea that women ordained abroad should be allowed to perform the ceremony in this country struck them as a dangerous farce.

The two-and-a-half-hour debate - staged in the university's utilitarian lecture hall overlooking an artificial lake populated with exotic ducks and geese - proved a famous victory for the traditionalists. The Synod threw out the measure unceremoniously; neither the House of Clergy nor the House of Laity produced the requisite two-thirds majority in favour. The lay vote was particularly significant, indicating a hardening of opinion against women priests in a constituency which had previously consistently backed the reform. The vote was a grievous reverse for the advocates of women priests, a bitter personal blow to McClatchey, who had introduced the motion, and a rebuff to Runcie, who had thrown his weight behind it. But one battle was not going to decide the war. If the most telling arguments came from the traditionalist ranks, it was because, on this occasion, they had logic on their side. It would indeed have been absurd to have decided to allow women priests ordained abroad to celebrate Communion at English altars (even under restricted conditions) before deciding whether or not to go ahead with legislation to give the same rights to women in this country. And those parts of the Anglican Church which had unilaterally ordained women priests without waiting for others to catch up could hardly complain if those others would not now play ball. The debate pivoted on the contributions of two women. McClatchey delivered strong opening and closing speeches in favour of her motion, but pleaded with die-hards to abstain (only six did) rather than issuing a clarion call to her troops. In contrast, Hewitt raised cheers and laughter when she described the proposals as 'intellectually indefensible, theologically reprehensible, as policy unworkable, as a contribution to Holy Communion, fantastical'. Gummer and Geldard also made pugnacious speeches. Runcie, bending over backwards to maintain harmonious relations with the liberals in America and Canada, warned against the Church of England adopting as isolationist, 'little Englander' policy, but his pleas fell on deaf ears. Expressing his dismay at the vote later, he said it would take some explaining away to his friends abroad.

As the traditionalist camp celebrated, despondent campaigners for women's ordination warned that the illegal services would go on. McClatchey recalls: 'I think that had the Standing Committee decided to hold the debate after the one on the McClean report, it would have taken half the opposition case away from them. They argued it was women priests through the back door. In fact, we were banging as hard as we could on the front door.' The gulf between the two sides was now wider than ever. 'I was aware how strongly they felt in a very negative way because at York that evening, in one of the college dining halls, a tableful of them ordered champagne and toasted each other in sheer celebration that they had defeated the Measure. I don't forget that sort of thing.'

The vote threw into even deeper uncertainty the outcome of the Tuesday debate on the McClean report, and the atmosphere at York reached a fever pitch of speculation and rumour. There were too many imponderables: what would happen, for example, to the traditionalist amendment which proposed the creation of a 'separate' Church of England? There were also profound theological matters at stake. The diocese had always been regarded as a basic unit of the Church and the diocesan bishop had always jealously guarded his autonomy within it. But, if some of the options in the McClean report were adopted, their freedom would be seriously curtailed. The question was: how much power would they be prepared to sacrifice in order to keep the peace? The report also seemed to give credence to the esoteric Anglo-Catholic belief that a bishop who ordained a woman priest somehow became 'tainted' with a form of episcopal 'Aids' because he had broken the apostolic succession, and therefore had to be shunned. In this view, divine authority was handed from bishop to bishop like a spiritual baton in a relay race begun by the apostles. Any bishop who ordained women, even if he had been properly consecrated, would be deemed to have dropped the baton and forfeited his God-given authority to perform the sacraments. This curious doctrine had been developed in the United States, where it had allowed the dissidents to divide the bishops into sheep and goats, those from whom they would accept ministry and those from whom they would not. The liberal bishops, in particular, found such a concept deeply distasteful. McClatchey argues: 'There is nothing special about about it being a male succession. Anyway, the whole apostolic thing is nonsense. It was never there at the beginning. In the beginning it was just a succession of teaching.' In fact, the 'tainted bishop' argument was not as widespread in this country as many of the MOW lobby made out. Many of the English traditionalists who threatened to shun those bishops who ordained women did so not because those bishops were considered 'tainted' but because they did not want to associate themselves with anyone who gave credence to the 'deception' that women could be priests.

When the debate on the McClean report arrived, a head-on collision between the express trains seemed inevitable. But once again Runcie and his senior colleagues were able to divert the juggernauts into the sidings. Runcie's *deus ex machina* took the form of an amendment proposing that the McClean report be taken over by the House of Bishops, which would in time produce its own report on the way forward for the legislation. The Archbishop told the Synod that the Church of England would hardly be the same body if some or all of the options in the report were acted upon. Tempers needed to be cool on both sides, he said. In itself, the report was not sufficient for wise judgements to be made. Slow progress had the merit of enabling change without bringing self-destruction on the Church. 'Some of the options would mean fundamental departure from episcopal government as the Church of England has known it since the time of St Augustine of Canterbury,' said Runcie, bringing all his historian's authority to bear. 'It becomes a moot point whether the ordination of women or the abolition of diocesan episcopacy would be the greater change.' He continued: 'To speak of parallel episcopates not in full communion is to legitimize schism. This would no longer be the Church of England as we have known it. How could we allow a situation where individual church members or groups decide who are real bishops and who are not? To reject the bishop is to reject the Church he represents.' Runcie added that at the root of some of the options was the view, apparently held by some, that bishops who had associated themselves with the ordination of women priests would no longer be valid ministers of the sacrament. To cheers he said: 'I find this an extraordinary attitude.' The rest of the debate was something of a formality. By a large majority, Synod members opted for the House of Bishops' compromise, and breathed a collective sigh of relief. For MOW, paradise had once again been postponed.

8

Balancing Act
(1986–87)

If the women priests dispute was to the Church of England what the question of Europe was to the Conservative Government, then the Tulsa affair was its Westland crisis. It led to a senior bishop breaking ranks and defying his Archbishop over an incident which was, in itself, insignificant but which, in the overheated atmosphere of the times, took on symbolic import. The improbable stage for what was to become a transatlantic drama was an unprepossessing, out-of-the-way parish at Broken Arrow in the American heartland of Oklahoma. Its origins, as with many *causes célèbres*, are somewhat obscure, but the catalyst was a legal battle between the outspoken, traditionalist rector of St Michael's, Father John Pasco, and his diocesan bishop over allegations of financial irregularities in the parish.

The struggle between Pasco and Bishop Gerald McAllister, a liberal, was symptomatic of the unrest still convulsing parts of the Episcopal Church in the wake of the first wave of ordinations. Relations between the two men were always prickly, but they deteriorated rapidly after claims were made that Pasco was encouraging parishioners to channel donations away from the diocese and into an unoffical trust. In 1985, Pasco was taken to a diocesan court and deposed, a move his supporters – including his congregation – regarded as a blatantly political manoeuvre by the liberal establishment to remove a thorn in its side. The sentence was upheld on appeal. McAllister then began civil proceedings to recover the St Michael's church building – little more than a Nissen hut – and the parish funds. Pasco and his parishioners were effectively homeless.

Pasco had first written to Leonard in 1984 and had spoken briefly to him in March 1986 during a convention of traditionalist clergy and bishops in Connecticut. In April, when the appeal court judgement came through, Pasco sent Leonard a cable: 'McAllister declared my deposition Friday. I refused to accept. Await your guidelines.' Leonard seized the opportunity for a grand gesture by 'adopting' what he considered to be an orphaned parish. His approach was characteristically legalistic. Although American bishops guarded as jealously as their English counterparts their autonomy within their dioceses, Leonard argued that St Michael's had, through the actions of the courts, become detached from the diocese of Oklahoma and the Episcopal Church. Historically, the Bishops of London had jurisdiction in the American colonies before the War of Independence. All he was now doing, he argued, was to come to the aid of a beleaguered congregation which had been deprived of any episcopal pastoral care and was in limbo. Leonard had, of course, intervened largely for political purposes; he suspected the parish was being punished for Pasco's traditionalist views. He then raised the stakes by promising to send the Bishop of Fulham, John Klyberg, to Tulsa to confirm parishioners on his behalf.

His stance provoked outrage. In the eyes of his detractors, he was cynically manipulating the letter of the law in order to flout its spirit. Whether or not his case was watertight, and many doubted it, he had certainly broken the unwritten law – that bishops should stick together. Leonard's own supporters questioned his judgement; his actions, they feared, would prove counter-productive because they would be portrayed as contrary to the very Church order he espoused. Even Garry Bennett, acting as an unofficial adviser to Runcie, said Leonard had no historical precedent. However romantic Broken Arrow sounded, it seemed hardly the best place for a last stand, and Leonard was no Custer. 'None of us even knew what he was up to,' says one. 'It was this sort of maverick individualism which often proved to be the bane of the Anglo-Catholic movement.' The American bishops, who argued that the parish remained under the jurisdiction of the diocese of Oklahoma, found Leonard's intervention in their internal affairs 'offensive in the extreme' and demanded that Runcie should act. At a tense meeting at Lambeth Palace in September, Runcie warned Leonard that Klyberg's visit would incur the wrath of the American bishops, and pleaded with him to reconsider. The appeal was only partially successful. On reflection, Leonard said, Runcie was right. He would not send Klyberg to Tulsa: he would go himself.

The American House of Bishops immediately went on to red alert. At a meeting in Texas, they demanded that any bishop who interfered in their internal affairs should be 'challenged, corrected and disciplined'. Leonard contrasted this sudden outbreak of disciplinarianism with the failure of the American bishops to take action against those colleagues who had illegally ordained women at Philadelphia, or against Elizabeth Canham, the woman priest who had unlawfully conducted a service in his diocese. If he had hoped for any sympathy from his own colleagues, however, he was to be disappointed. At a chilly meeting of the Church of England's House of Bishops in October, a week before he was due to depart for Tulsa, he found himself in a minority of one. Undaunted, Leonard visited Tulsa at the end of October to conduct a confirmation service. Returning to a uniformly hostile reception, he had an hour and a half meeting with Runcie in early November. Their theological differences were deep: Runcie emphasized the importance of collegiality, of bishops acting together; Leonard said collegiality had been destroyed by the unilateral action of individual Anglican Churches. The cracks were widening.

'He didn't help matters,' recalls Runcie.

The case was presented that he was going to provide confirmation for people who otherwise were not going to get it. I said you must go with the goodwill of the bishop of the diocese. I thought he was going with the goodwill of the bishop but, as it turned out, he clearly wasn't. I tried to make his going conditional upon getting the goodwill of the bishop. That's not an unusual thing – we shall have plenty of it with these flying bishops. When I eventually went to Tulsa years later I found it laughable that it had been so inflated by the press and the traditionalists. It seemed to me to be a congregation more interested in disobeying the bishop than of maintaining Catholic integrity.

Leonard, unsurprisingly, views it differently.

I have no regrets. People in America told me that it was the first time that anybody was prepared to challenge the official line. Although I can't say I am very happy with the general outcome now, it did mark a significant event, someone actually doing something about those who were seeking to undermine the Catholic tradition of the Church. When I had a press conference on my return from Tulsa, someone asked me, did you break the law? I said no, I didn't break the law. I upset the club.

Any collateral damage that Leonard's would-be pre-emptive strike might have inflicted was, however, offset by the blunder perpetrated by the supporters of women priests a few weeks before his trip. Joyce Bennett, by now retired from Hong Kong and working as a chaplain to the Chinese Anglican community in London, was invited by MOW to celebrate Communion at a private and, it was hoped, confidential service at the organization's annual general meeting in a hall in Church House. It was a sign of the pro-women lobby's mounting frustration at their lack of progress, and MOW had got away with similar services at previous AGMs. Despite the Synod's ruling on women ordained abroad, many still regarded the law as ambiguous, and many of them thought that a private service on unconsecrated ground would not constitute a breach, particularly as Bishop Peter Selby of Kingston and Alan Webster were among 40 clergy who took Communion. But when news of the event came out, opponents of women priests gleefully exploited the situation to deflect the heat from Leonard. The legal justifications produced by MOW were, after all, as tendentious as those used by the Bishop of London. Runcie ordered an immediate inquiry and issued a statement saying he was 'dismayed to hear of this disregard for the clearly understood present regulations of the Church of England.' Oswald Clark, the Anglo-Catholic vice-chairman of the corporation of Church House, even sought to embroil the Queen in the affair, saying the service had been an affront to the monarch because the room in which it had been held came within her jurisdiction. MOW was unrepentant; Margaret Webster, its secretary, said the organization planned to encourage sympathetic parishes to 'adopt' women priests ordained overseas and invite them to celebrate in England.

Bennett was called in to see Runcie in his study at Lambeth Palace. She recalls:

> I had a formal letter from Bishop Ronald Gordon, the chief of staff at Lambeth, inquiring as to whether this rumour about a celebration was true, and a little hand-written note from Runcie saying, 'I'm afraid I have to do this but I don't really agree with it.' I went to have tea with Runcie and we sat in front of a log fire. He had a great file on his desk and he said, these are all legal reflections on what happened, but he never opened it because they obviously all disagreed with each other. He wanted me to say I would never celebrate in England again, but I refused. What about emergencies, if I was called to the bedside of a dying parishioner? He saw the point of that. So eventually I wrote to say that I promised never again to celebrate in Church House.

Runcie recalls being somewhat firmer than that.

> I did forbid Joyce Bennett quite clearly and said I couldn't countenance it. With Graham Leonard I did much the same thing. Both of them had their own constituencies and naturally in those constituencies I had a villainous reputation, but I don't regret what I did then, nor do I think it was inconsistent with the line which I was generally taking of holding the Church of England together according to its traditions. Now it is becoming plain that it can only nourish those traditions by accepting this step of ordaining women.

The twin affairs overshadowed the November Synod, but a debate on them – prompted by a call for both Leonard and MOW to apologize for their actions – failed to get off the ground. Runcie said the Synod should not debate the issues without all the facts to hand, but criticized bishops who 'offended against collegiality'. Leonard said that having promised to confirm the candidates in Tulsa, it was 'quite unthinkable' that last-minute pleas should have led him to say 'I'm sorry, I'm not coming.' The contribution made by McClatchey, one of the organizers of the Church House service, was, however, to have more profound ramifications. Her conciliatory speech – in which she said the service had been planned in good faith but if lawyers decided it had been illegal 'our judgement could be said to have been in error' – provoked acrimonious behind-the-scenes recriminations in the pro-women camp.

'Some of our own supporters were furious that I had admitted that, had I known it was illegal, I wouldn't have done it,' she explains.

But I certainly wouldn't have asked Joyce Bennett to celebrate if I had had any idea it would cause that sort of rumpus. We gave ourselves the benefit of the doubt in a very grey area. I can still remember that some of them up in the public gallery during my speech were really disgusted that I hadn't gone to town much more. They wanted me to get on a high horse of principle. A group formed the St Hilda Community soon after that. I think they felt that MOW was not going to be radical enough and confrontational enough and the situation demanded that attitude. I remember at the MOW AGM the following year, we invited the Archbishop of York to celebrate. I wrote to him and asked him to take the opportunity to spell out what was his understanding of the law, which he did. This made some of the MOW women very angry. There was a counter-service which took place outside because they were not prepared for him to celebrate. There was a great anti-man wave going through some in those days and they were not prepared to accept the sacrament at the hands of a man. That is why St Hilda's filled a need. There were some pretty damaged women around.

St Hilda's, whose founding members included Monica Furlong and Suzanne Fageol, an American priest from Chicago, as well as a handful of male sympathizers, held regular Sunday services in St Benet's, a small chapel attached to the chaplaincy of Queen Mary College, an East End offshoot of London University. MOW was ambivalent towards the radical new group, which used New Age-style feminist liturgies in which God was referred to as Mother and her. Conservative members of MOW feared the St Hilda Community could prove counter-productive to the cause. While never expelling the members of the community, MOW distanced itself from their activities, which included the production of a non-sexist prayer book (disowned by Lambeth Palace and condemned by some as blasphemous) that included an alternative version of the Lord's Prayer which began: 'Beloved our Father and Mother, in whom is heaven.' Many of the group's unconventional Communion services were celebrated by Fageol and were therefore illegal in the Church of England. Initially, London diocesan officials turned a Nelsonian eye, but in October 1989, news of the group's dubious worship became public and Leonard was forced to crack down. He sent a letter to Fageol in which he 'expected and requested' her to desist from the services. But, after a vote, about 40 members of the community defiantly went ahead with the service; the congregation, as usual, squatted on the floor around the altar or danced in a ring, using a liturgy which referred to God as her. Despite a flurry of media attention and a spate of solicitor's letters (Fageol joked that while Jesus thought trespassers should be forgiven, Leonard preferred the legal services of Winckworth and Pemberton), the community returned the following week, this time to find the doors of the chapel locked to them. In bitter cold, watched by television crews and policemen, Fageol celebrated in the car park outside. But the community's moral victory was short lived: from then on it was forced to use a Methodist chapel down the road.

February 1986 saw another ponderous step towards the ordination of women priests. The House of Bishops had produced its promised first report (a second report would be published the following year) on the theological principles that should underpin the women priests legislation, and submitted it for the approval of the Synod. The report concluded that safeguards should be included to protect the interests of traditionalists, even though these would entail the diocesan bishops giving up some of their prized autonomy. Crucially, however, it went on to say these safeguards 'should be seen as an interim measure'. Any notion that the Church could formally and permanently split into two, or that traditionalist bishops could bar women from their diocese indefinitely, was ruled out. The report instead proposed that a bishop who was in post at the time the legislation came into force would have the right to declare that he would not ordain a woman or employ a woman priest in his diocese. During his term in office, therefore, his diocese would become a 'no go' zone for women priests. His successor would not, however, enjoy a similar right. The report said that clergy should retain their traditional veto over who could celebrate in their churches. But it added a new safeguard: parochial church councils, it suggested, should have the additional right, irrespective of the views of the bishop or the incumbent, to decide that women priests would not be acceptable in the parish. The House of Bishops' report – with one eye on what Parliament would find acceptable – also agreed that compensation should be paid to clergy resigning over the issue, but said the 'golden handshake' should be contained in a separate, but linked, piece of legislation.

Many supporters of women priests thought the package was outragous. They wanted a simple, single clause measure, giving women the same rights as men. That, they argued, was the only just solution; the dissentient minority (34 per cent of regular churchgoers, according to an opinion poll published in December 1986) who did not like it could live with it or quit the Church. It was also a simple solution, one which would avoid the complexities, fudges, and theological contortions promised by the report. But the traditionalist camp was equally horrified. Many of them believed that the safeguards did not go nearly far enough, and that the cumulative effect of the proposals would, over time, drive them from the Church. Under the proposals, diocesan bishops appointed *after* the legislation came into force would not enjoy the same rights as those already in office, and would not be able to declare their dioceses to be 'no go' areas for women priests. The implication was that no new diocesan bishop could be appointed from the traditionalist constituency, unless, of course, he swallowed his principles and agreed to ordain women priests. And when those traditionalist bishops already in place had retired, there would be no 'safe havens' for opponents of women priests or senior spokemen representing them in the House of Bishops. The career ladder for Anglo-Catholic clergy would also be snatched away, deterring many would-be priests from entering the Church. It would only be a matter of time before the Anglo-Catholic wing would wither away, a rump of bitter clergymen and a few pockets of dissenting parishes. The much-vaunted comprehensiveness of the Church of England would be destroyed. It was a demoralizing prospect.

Despite the objections of the two extremes, there was little chance that the Synod would reject the Bishops' package: it seemed to square the circle, to adequately protect the consciences of opponents while maintaining the essential integrity of the Church. It was a significant step forward; for the first time, the Synod had been presented with a blueprint for legislation which commanded a broad consensus. Once the legislative process had been started, it would run to its own timetable and acquire its own momentum; so much time and so many expectations would be tied up in it that it would be almost impossible to stop. Geldard recalls: 'The decision to prepare legislation represented the opening of the floodgates. The ploy of supporters of women priests was always to say, "this is not the crunch, don't get over excited". Then when the crunch came, the ploy was to say, "we've come this far, we can't stop now".' In the February Synod debate, Runcie seemed to be deploying these tactics when he said he regretted the premature panic which had greeted the publication of the report. Not only did it not tell opponents of women priests to get out of the Church, but accepting it was not the same thing as endorsing the ordination of women priests, which remained a long way off, he said. 'It is therefore a little early to be taking the tarpaulins off the lifeboats, or even signalling to other shipping to stand by to take on some of the passengers.'

Leonard was, however, polishing up the semaphore. Though a

signatory to the unanimous report, he told the Synod that an acceptance of its proposals would fundamentally alter the structure and
doctrine of the Church and he would have to look elsewhere. He
justified his schismatic stance by seizing on a passage he had been
largely responsible for inserting; it said that those who could not in
conscience stay in the Church must 'explore other ways'. Following
the debate – in which the House of Bishops' report was received by
317 to 145 (with eight bishops voting against) – Leonard said he
would begin 'taking soundings' to determine the feasibility of
opponents of women priests allying themselves with the Roman
Catholic or Orthodox Churches. 'It seems to me that we have been
given the green light,' he said. We cannot wait forever.' The seeds of
what has come to be known as the 'Roman option' were sown.

Within a few weeks, the pro-ordination camp was rejoicing again
as the first women were ordained deacons. After a protracted
process, and despite last minute hitches, the legislation had been
finally enacted at the February Synod. The first group of 15 women
to receive their clerical collars and the right to be titled 'The
Reverend' gathered for an emotional but restrained ceremony in a
hushed Canterbury cathedral at the end of February, presided over
by Runcie. On the eve of the historic service, Runcie said the admission of women into holy orders for the first time would 'switch the
atmosphere' of both the Church of England and the whole country.
After it, the newly ordained deacon Margaret Mascall said the
transformation was already underway. 'The atmosphere was so
powerful. It's not just something enclosed within these four walls.
It's going to fizz.'

More than 700 women deacons were ordained up and down the
country over the next few months. Ironically Leonard, who
attacked the Church of England for 'simply following fashion' in its
desire to admit women priests, was among the first diocesan
bishops to ordain women deacons, albeit amid controversy. The
service was boycotted by the Bishop of Edmonton, Brian Masters,
and nearly two dozen diehard clergymen protested by simultaneously holding prayer meetings in their churches. But, despite a few
incidents in rural parishes, the widespread friction forecast by some
failed to materialize, and women clergy – who were now entitled to

preside at all the essential 'rites of passage' ceremonies, baptisms, weddings and funerals – were rapidly incorporated into the blood-stream of the Church. Deacon Ruth Wintle became the first female honorary canon when she was installed at Worcester cathedral in the summer. Meanwhile the Methodist Church, with which many Anglicans still wanted to unite, elected the Revd Kathleen Richardson as its first woman district chairman, its equivalent of a bishop.

But movement was not all in one direction. In August 1987, the General Synod of the Anglican Church in Australia narrowly defeated moves to ordain women priests there. Tearful, banner-wielding women campaigners gathered outside St Andrew's cathe-dral in Sydney after the vote to sing 'We Shall Be Ordained' to the tune of 'We Shall Overcome'. They saw the setback as temporary, albeit painful. In the Roman Catholic Church, however, the nascent women's rights movement was once again shown a red light by the Pope. The expectations of campaigners – who ranged from liberal Jesuit theologians to nuns in the feminist St Joan's Alliance – had been heightened by the October Synod of 216 Roman Catholic cardinals and bishops in Rome, an event which occurred only once every four years. The topic under discussion was ostensibly the role of the laity, but the barely concealed agenda of many bishops was the role of women. American and English cardinals – including Hume – were particularly sympathetic to the case for enhancing female rights, and were confident they could improve women's status by persuading the Pope to open to them all ecclesiastical functions short of the priesthood. After three weeks of intense debate behind closed doors in the Vatican, they seemed to have won a concession; a clause proposing that women be admitted to such male-only preserves as altar servers, readers and deacons won majority support and was included in the draft proposals presented to the Pope. When the final document was published a few days later, however, the clause had been mysteriously dropped, and, to the anger of the Americans in particular, only vague generalizations about the role of women remained. Many of the delegates were privately furious at what they regarded as the worst sort of under-hand papal interference, but publicly they bit their tongues. Vatican sources suggested that papal aides had removed the offending clause to avoid causing difficulties to bishops working in Third World communities in which men were still the unchallenged leaders. But many delegates detected the personal hand of Pope John Paul II. The Pope's 195-page response to the Synod, *Christifideles Laici*, which was issued in January 1989, acknowledged the role of women in the Church, but made few concessions to those who wanted equal status with men (though the ban on girl altar servers was dropped in 1994).

In the coming months, Runcie must have wished he enjoyed such papal immunity from public criticism. Until the end of 1987, the Church of England's debate on women priests had, superficially at least, been conducted with a fair degree of tolerance and restraint; behind the exterior, however, boiled a seething mass of bitterness, frustration, anger and resentment. The traditionalist minority felt increasingly beleaguered. They believed they were being marginalized by the liberal establishment, that able clergy from their ranks were not being promoted because their views were unfashionable. While such suspicions were most deeply harboured by those who felt they had been unfairly passed over, feelings ran much more deeply than that. Beneath all the Trollopian power struggles, there was a profound fear that the abyss between the conservatives and the liberals was yawning so wide that the Church could disappear into it. A growing number worried that the Lambeth Conference in 1988 – which had to tackle the issue of women bishops – could prove the nemesis for Anglicanism. They blamed weak leadership by Runcie for failing to counter the corroding influence of liberalism.

The dissenters' *cri de coeur* came in the improbable form of the unsigned preface of the *Crockford's Clerical Directory*, an annual publication listing the names and addresses of Anglican clergy. The tradition of a gently acerbic preface, written by a senior cleric behind a veil of anonymity, was well established, but the diatribe issued on 3 December 1987 departed from the norm by launching a grave and sustained assault on the Church leadership, and Runcie in particular. It accused Runcie of prevarication and of 'nailing his colours to the fence'. The anonymous author added that the

Archbishop lacked firm principles and had surrounded himself 'with men who have nothing to prevent them following what they think is the wish of the moment' by packing the Bench of Bishops with like-minded liberals. He also attacked the liberal line on a range of issues, from homosexuality among the clergy to women priests, and warned that the Church would be pulled apart unless its more extreme elements, such as the American bishops, exercised self restraint.

The preface precipitated one of the most serious crises ever to confront the Church of England. Although Runcie maintained a dignified silence, other bishops attacked the character of the unknown author, fuelling a media hunt to unmask him. While many of the preface's barbs would have been commonplace around college high tables – indeed Runcie was well aware of them himself – the crime was to have made them public. The tragic denouement – Gareth Bennett killed himself by running a hose from his exhaust pipe into his car after persistently denying he was the author – plunged the Church into a period of self-doubt and despair. For a time, it seemed as though the pendulum might swing back to the traditionalists as people digested the implications of the preface: for the first time for decades in the Church of England, religious beliefs had become a matter of life and death. Austin won applause for a speech in the General Synod debate in February 1988, in which he implored the liberals to end their 'contempt' for the traditionalists. Others hoped the preface might effectively form the agenda for the 1988 Lambeth Conference. But, despite a few promotions designed to restore the perceived imbalance (Austin, for example, was appointed Archdeacon of York), the traditionalists made few real gains in the wake of the affair. Indeed, their influence was probably diminished; the liberals had survived the worst that could be thrown at them.

Runcie dismisses suggestions that Bennett's suicide had deeply wounded him. 'I was quite a good friend of Garry's,' he says.

> We were quite open in disagreement. I knew he was not satis-
> fied. I was sorry about the episode, and I tried to pray for
> Garry, but there were many other things happening. There

was a lot of treaclish hypocrisy around the Church which I did find unpleasant, people saying 'we are behind you', but they were really only behind you if you survived. There were so many mixed motives that might have led to Garry's death that it was difficult to pinpoint it as a simple cry of pain that the liberals had won the day and the traditionalists were not being heard.

Campaigners for the cause of women priests tended to see Bennett's suicide as a one-off personal tragedy rather than a symptom of a creeping malaise. Bennett was, after all, a lonely repressed homosexual. 'It was all a sideshow, except that our opponents tried to blame the women priests issue, saying, look how far you have gone,' comments McClatchey. 'I had one letter which said, now you have blood on your hands, perhaps you are satisfied. I was very hurt by the way the opposition made political capital of it.' Those on the other side of the divide saw the reaction of senior bishops to what they regarded as Bennett's accurate analysis in a very different light. 'It showed up a sickness in the Church,' says Geldard. 'It showed its tooth and claw. It showed a viciousness that wishes to protect its own, a viciousness which does not mind what price is paid to achieve its end. The establishment couldn't appeal to charity or love. It had to come in with the iron boot.'

9

The Lambeth Walk

(1988–89)

As the 1988 Lambeth Conference drew near, the heavyweight artillery was heaved on to the battlefield. In February, 47 traditionalist bishops from across the world, including seven English diocesans, issued a statement warning that the consecration of women bishops would split Anglicanism in two. In May, 141 liberal bishops, including eight from England, returned the salvo by throwing their full support behind women bishops. Attempting to make his voice heard above the din, Runcie used a lecture in New York to admonish some of the more gung ho, liberal provinces, saying that if they did not exercise self restraint, they could find themselves being forced to renounce some of their prized autonomy. He even quoted, favourably, a section of Bennett's notorious preface to bolster his argument. It was a theme he was to return to time and again in the coming months as part of his strategy to put a brake on further disruptive changes within the Anglican Communion by trying to shift power from the provinces towards its more responsible collective leadership.

But a fortnight before the 525 bishops of the worldwide Church congregated at Canterbury in mid July, the Church of England had its own critical decision to make: whether to begin the lengthy and divisive process of legislating for women priests. When it met in York in early July, the General Synod had before it, for the first time, the draft Priests (Ordination of Women) Measure and two accompanying canons, designed to legalize the ordination of women as priests (but not their consecration as bishops) within a framework of safeguards for dissenters. Bishops who were opposed to change would have the right to make three separate declarations, the combined effect of which was to bar women priests from their dioceses – to the distress of those parishes that wanted a female vicar. Bishops who favoured the ordination of women, on the other hand, would have to relinquish full control of their dioceses; under the proposed safeguards, they would have to respect the wishes of those parochial church councils which exercised their rights to ring-fence their parishes against women priests. Again, many proponents of female ordination argued for a one clause Measure designed to put women on par with men at a stroke. They felt the safeguards would restrict the rights of women priests to minister in large tracts of the country and should be dispensed with in their entirety. But if the consciences of the bishops could not contemplate such a radical step – particularly as they knew they would ultimately have to steer the legislation through Parliament – they were deeply alarmed at some of the small print of the draft legislation. This gave traditionalist bishops far more powerful safeguards than the House of Bishops had envisaged in its report. Clause 2 of the Measure, as it then stood, proposed that diocesan bishops should have the right to block both the ordination and operation of women priests in their dioceses. But whereas the House of Bishops report recommended that this safeguard should only apply to diocesan bishops in office when the legislation was finally enacted, giving the provision a relatively short shelf life, the draft legislation included no such limitation: any diocesan bishop, whenever he was appointed, could enjoy the full range of rights.

For the majority, the consequences of this were intolerable: they accepted that the Church of England would have to be split into two for a short, interim period in order to accommodate the traditionalists, but, as it stood, the draft legislation would entrench schism permanently. The most traditionalist dioceses could ensure they were led by a succession of sympathetic bishops. Thus they would be able to exclude women priests indefinitely. Permanent Anglo-Catholic ghettos would be created which would not only stand in contradiction to the will of the majority view of the Church that women could be validly ordained, but also form a constant reminder to women priests that significant areas of the country were closed to them. While the traditionalists felt that such legislation was their only long-term hope of survival, the majority of the bishops were aware that such a situation would create an 'open wound in the Church which could never be healed.'

Nearly as contentious was the second, accompanying piece of draft legislation, the Ordination of Women (Financial Provisions) Measure. This provided for 'golden handshakes' for clergy resigning over the issue, and it was criticized not only by those who saw no need for compensation at all, but also by traditionalists who felt it was mean and niggardly. Under its provisions, the average pay-off would be over £30,000, but traditionalists saw this as paltry recompense for losing their homes and livelihoods. Many held a contrary view. One senior Church Commissioner robustly compared the position of the dissenters with that of a nuclear industry worker who decided to resign after discovering that his plant was secretly manufacturing nuclear weapons. 'That person wouldn't receive any compensation,' was his comment.

The July Synod debate on the draft legislation showed how nervously the Church of England was approaching the prospect of another protracted and divisive instalment of the women priest saga. Many thought any decision should be postponed until after the Lambeth Conference. Although the principle of the ordination of women still commanded the support of the vast majority, the draft legislation, with its controversial safeguards, was a different matter. Even the opponents were divided over tactics: some wanted to carry on objecting to women priests in principle while others wanted to switch the attack on to the legislation itself. In the event the draft legislation squeezed through, but only by a slim margin. In fact, for the first time since the Synod first voted on the issue in the 1970s, it failed to achieve a two-thirds majority – the threshold it would ultimately require to gain final approval – in any of the three Houses, bishops, clergy or laity. A growing number feared that the Church was embarking on a bitter and draining internal struggle – it would be at least another three years before the draft legislation had cleared all its hurdles – without any realistic prospect that it would be finally enacted.

Runcie's hesitations reflected the anxieties of many. The profound theological gulf between the bishops had been exposed in the House of Bishops' second report, which had been published a few weeks earlier. The report explored the arguments on either side without even attempting to come to a conclusion, a fact which had angered Leonard who saw it as another example of 'theological levity'. From the traditionalists' perspective, however, the report had finally laid to rest the troublesome spirit of the 1975 resolution that there were 'no fundamental objections' to women priests.

But Runcie's own views – and those of a growing number in the 'centre' – were perceptibly shifting in favour of ordaining women. He says now:

> The American Church should have proceeded with more consultation, more concensus, than it did. But the shift did not occur just because there was pressure from outside but because there were good arguments. There was a great deal of interaction between the liberal and the traditionalist arguments and, in the eyes of a great many people, the liberal arguments won. There is little evidence of major movements over to the 'stop the women' camp compared to the number of movements over to the acceptance of women's ordination. The process of acceptability does not come from any hidden liberal agenda. It comes from open, honest argument and a perception of what is happening in the world.

In the General Synod debates Runcie had made clear that, for him, it was now not a question of if but when. He strongly counselled patience. Neither the bishops' second report nor the draft legislation, pointed to increased consensus, he argued. The proposals – particularly those dealing with the safeguards for traditionalists – seemed to be a kind of legislative schism 'which would endanger the episcopal and pastoral character of the Church of England as we know it,' he said. But the Synod was in no mood to listen to faint-hearted speeches. Although the Measure was heartily disliked by both sides, the majority of members was ultimately swayed by the argument that it could still be altered when it reached its revision stage, and to curtail the debate at this stage, before the dioceses had an opportunity to examine it, would amount to 'irresponsible fiddling'. The voting was, however, hardly a decisive endorsement of the draft legislation, a clear sign that trouble lay ahead. The House of Bishops voted 28 for and 21 against; the House of Clergy 137 for and 102 against; and the House of Laity 134 for and 93 against.

Just 11 days after the General Synod in York, Runcie was opening the Lambeth Conference in Canterbury – the biggest test of his tenure in office. The prophets of doom had had a field day, predicting the final disintegration of the worldwide Church from an ecclesiastical Commonwealth to little more than a loosely-linked federation. Like cricket, Anglicanism had been exported to all parts of the Empire at a time when there was no question about who was in charge. But now the former colonials had adapted what had been a very British form of religion to their own native conditions and resented the interference of the mother Church. The liberal New Zealanders were particularly scathing about what they perceived as the Church of England's air of superiority, and the worldwide structure was beginning to creak. But Runcie had done his ground-work; his travels around the world, persuading the 27 autonomous 'branch' Churches that it was better to be in the club than out, were to bear fruit. He had successfully persuaded the liberal Americans – the most assertively self-governing – to postpone consecrating a woman bishop until after the conference, but he was well aware they would not wait much longer than that. He also knew that, to isolate the diehard traditionalists, he needed to keep the moderate conservative provinces on board by tightening his grip over the more gung-ho liberals. In his opening address to the conference, Runcie echoed his New York lecture by telling the bishops that the future of the worldwide Church lay between provincial independence (and fragmentation) and interdependence (and more centralized authority). 'It would be a gentle, even genteel, fragmentation – that much of Englishness still remains – and it would not be instant,' he said. 'As I have said, the Communion is not about to disappear tomorrow. But decisive choice is before us. Do we want the Anglican Communion? And if we do, what are we going to do about it?' By the end of the conference, the argument was going his way: the bishops voted to give greater status to the regular meetings of the 27 primates, a sort of college of Cardinals without a Pope.

The atmosphere at the start of the three-week conference was nevertheless palpably tense. Barbara Harris, by then tipped to become Anglicanism's first women bishop, flew in from Philadelphia to join other campaigning women priests – including the very first, Florence Tim Oi Li, and the black American Nan Peete, one of the speakers – in an act denounced as provocative by the traditionalists camp. About 140 liberal American and Canadian bishops upset even middle-of-the-road opinion by refusing, in a clumsy gesture designed to demonstrate solidarity with the feminist constituency, to preside at any services during the conference. The small but vocal traditionalist contingent – made up of bishops from Texas to Papua New Guinea – held surreptitious briefings for the press in campus bars. Rumours abounded, dark threats were uttered and brinkmanship was practised by both sides: while the Americans threatened to consecrate a woman whatever Lambeth decided, Leonard and other traditionalists threatened to sever their links with any bishop (or Archbishop) who participated in or even supported such consecrations. Leonard's most uncomfortable moment occurred after Peete had delivered her presentation to the conference in which she described her experiences as a rector in a parish in Indianapolis. As she sat a few feet away from him on the same platform, he was asked whether or not she was a priest. 'I don't think that is a fair question,' he stumbled. 'I am not prepared to say she is and I am not prepared to say she is not.'

Runcie, meanwhile, maintained a precarious balance on his diplomatic high-wire: he would, he told friends, recognize the Church's first woman bishop as validly consecrated within her own province, but would not countenance her operating in England, where her ministry could not be deemed legal. Meanwhile Leonard and Spong, whose brand of liberalism put even Jenkins in the shade, resumed their Punch and Judy show. Leonard opened the bout by accusing his rival of rejecting the teachings of the Bible and promoting homosexual 'marriages'. An undaunted Spong, who was photographed in his track suit jogging around the Kent university campus, denounced Leonard for trying to 'blackmail' the Church over women bishops. Spong characterized Leonard's threat to sever relations with liberal bishops as being like 'a little kid saying I'm going to take my marbles and go home.' Despite the vitriol, the two men actually got on quite amicably when they met face to face. 'I met Spong at Lambeth and I said we must have a talk, let's have dinner this evening,' recalls Leonard.

> We went to the refectory there and we had a long talk and we went on to a bar and continued late into the night. The next morning the presiding bishop of Ecusa, Edmund Browning, said to me 'I saw you talking to Jack Spong last night'. I said 'yes, for most of the evening'. He said 'but you don't agree with him'. I said that was why I was talking to him. He said 'in America we don't talk to people we disagree with'. That was very revealing. Then he said, 'I saw you walking across the campus with the women priest who was there, Nan Peete, but you don't recognise her. 'No', I said, 'but I can still talk to her'.

The formal proceedings started with the by now ritual pleas for caution from the Roman Catholic and Orthodox Churches. They had little impact; the majority felt the Anglican debate over women priests had gone too far to be diverted by considerations about wider Christian unity. Anyway, Rome and Constantinople seemed to be crying wolf; if their objections were really profound, why had they not already broken off relations? In fact, the Lambeth bishops subsequently endorsed the first ARCIC report, which had been drawn up by the official joint commission of Roman Catholic and Anglican theologians. The report was widely praised as a milestone in bridging the theological gulf that had divided the two Churches since the Reformation, particularly over their understanding of the nature of Communion and the ministry. In fact, the document was full of ambiguities (the word 'transubstantiation' was used just once, in a footnote). In terms of reunion, however, much rested on both Churches being able to accept the report. Now that the Anglicans had done just that, the ball was in the Vatican's court once again. In the minds of many of the Lambeth bishops, therefore, the two projects – women's ordination and reunion with Rome – were far from mutually exclusive.

The official resolution on women bishops was – like all Lambeth resolutions – privately compiled by a small group of bishops representing a range of opinions. The group, which included both Leonard and Browning, had studied the report drawn up by Archbishop Grindrod which developed the ancient concept of 'reception', a bizarre-sounding theological idea which was nevertheless seized on by Church leaders as a way of keeping dialogue going between the warring parties. Under Grindrod's proposals, the innovation of women bishops would be 'received' by the Church on a provisional basis: if the experiment was contrary to the will of God, the Church could ultimately reject it (though how was never explained). The advantage of the idea was that those doubtful about women bishops could feel that a final decision had not quite been made; the reality was that, once embarked on, the experiment was effectively irreversible. As one traditionalist bishop put it: 'It is not easy to get the toothpaste back into the tube.'

The notion of reception nevertheless underpinned the official resolution, the wording of which was approved by all the members of the Mission and Ministry group, including, significantly, Leonard. The resolution, which recognized the inevitability of women bishops, was itself anodyne and there was never any doubt that it would be approved when the whole conference voted on it the following month. The five-part resolution asked bishops to 'exercise courtesy and maintain communications' with each other, however badly relations became strained. It called Runcie to set up another commission to 're-examine' the relationships between individual Anglican provinces, and to draw up guidelines to safeguard traditionalists. Leonard, meanwhile, pointed out that the resolution nowhere said that the consecration of women was theologically valid, a somewhat paltry triumph in the circumstances. But the traditionalist camp still hoped to win more. The conservative Evangelical Archbishop of Sydney, Dr Donald Robinson, tabled a 'private members' resolution calling on provinces to 'refrain' from consecrating a woman, at least until the Archbishop of Canterbury's new commission could report back. This unofficial resolution served two purposes. In the unlikely event that it was adopted, it would have the effect of isolating those Americans who jumped the gun. If it failed, it would still demonstrate the strength of the opposition.

On 1 August 1988, the eve of the conference debate on women bishops, the pro-ordination camp received support from an improbable quarter – Margaret Thatcher. Speaking to journalists as she left for a trip to the Far East, she said: 'I personally think that there will be women in the priesthood, and I do not myself find it at odds with the Christian doctrine.' She would have been delighted with the outcome of the following day. After an interminable debate in the university's main lecture theatre, the conference overwhelmingly approved the official resolution, paving the way for the consecration of Anglicanism's first woman bishop. The voting was 423 in favour to 28 against, a majority of 395. The arguments from both sides during the three and a half hour debate were fierce, though there was never much doubt about the result. Bishop Ralph Hatendi from Zimbabwe, Africa, said women bishops would be totally unacceptable in his country. 'Are male beings jealous that Mary was chosen to be the mother of God?' he asked. 'It is God in the male being that was sacrificed for us and it is logical that a male being is the representative of Christ at the altar, by divine commission or divine providence.' Bishop Willie Pwaisho of Malaita, Melanesia, was even more robust. 'If women for the episcopate and women for the priesthood has come as a result of women's liberation, then I think it is Satanic, and we should take great care before we decide.' But Archbishop Desmond Tutu of Cape Town, supporting the resolution, said he did so out of his 'concern for liberation and justice. I couldn't say that I had that kind of commitment and then agree with the discrimination of people on the basis of their gender.' Bishop John Walker of Washington reminded the conference that not so long ago black men were not considered 'human enough' to be bishops. 'The very same things that have been said over the centuries by white men about black men and black people in general are now being said about women,' he said. 'All are one in him, and I believe the moment has come in our life together when we must proceed, at least as provinces, with what we believe the Holy Spirit is calling us to do.'

The second resolution – tabled by Archbishop Robinson – was, potentially, far more explosive. The traditionalists hoped the conservative African and Asian bishops would join them in their revolt against the progressive Churches and vote *en masse* with them. Introducing his resolution, Robinson said: 'I am all for an ambulance at the bottom of the cliff to deal with whatever situation may arise in the coming days, which is what is proposed by the main resolution. But we can do more. We may not be in a position to erect a fence, but at least we can display a well-marked warning sign at the top of the cliff.' But Edmund Browning said that in his province there were more than 1,000 ordained women. 'This resolution ignores the maturity we have achieved and the gifts we have been given and shared,' he argued. 'I believe it invites anarchy and would usher in disunity.' The vote on the second resolution was held by secret ballot. After agonizing minutes, the result was announced: 187 for to 227 against. The resolution was defeated – albeit by a majority of just 90. The conservative African vote had failed to materialize; the traditionalist camp was in disarray.

In September, the diocese of Massachusetts elected the 58-year-old Barbara Harris to be its suffragan and the world's first Anglican women bishop. Though not unexpected, the news sent a jolt throughout the worldwide Church. While the choice of the gritty, articulate former oil executive was perfect for an American diocese eager to show itself to be free of prejudice, it was seen by many elsewhere as a provocative act. Not only was Harris a woman – and black – but she was a divorcee and a supporter of radical causes and gay rights. Her consecration on 11 February 1989 was as much a black American celebration as a religious ceremony; highly charged and even occasionally raucous, it was as far removed from the restrained grandeur of Canterbury cathedral as can be imagined. The three-hour televised service, which was attended by members of MOW and a few retired English bishops, was staged in Boston's Olympia-style convention centre, the concrete and steel edifice more akin to an aircraft hangar than a church. Gospel choirs sang, speeches were made and the 8,500-strong congregation swayed, clapped, cheered, wept and released balloons. A long, standing ovation followed the high point of the service when 55 purple-clad bishops formed a knot around Harris and, like some vast sea anemone, converged to place their hands upon her. Attempts by two opponents of women priests to halt the proceedings were greeted with a chorus of boos and hisses and were waved away by Browning, who was conducting the service. But outside the centre, emotions were also running on octane. One American tradition-alist, the Revd Harold McElwain, rector of Old St Paul's in Portland, Maine, held a 'requiem' service for the Episcopal Church; above his church building flew the Episcopal flag upside down and at half-mast as 'a sign of distress – an SOS.' Above it he flew the Jolly Roger as a sign that 'the liberals are pirating the Church.' He was not alone in his dismay.

In England, the reaction was predictably mixed. While Runcie attempted to remain above the verbal volleying like a tennis umpire adjudicating at Wimbledon, supporters danced in the aisles at a celebration service at St James's church, Piccadilly. A number of bishops (who had kept away from the consecration at Runcie's request) expressed delight; Rogerson, a leading member of MOW, said that the consecration was a sign that 'God's Kingdom includes within it both women and men.' Leonard, however, threw down the gauntlet: in a statement that seemed designed to precipitate schism, he declared that he could neither recognize the validity of Harris's ministry, nor that of any priest she ordained. He also severed relations (by declaring himself 'out of communion') with all those bishops who had participated in her consecration, including Browning. In a private meeting with Runcie on the eve of the November Synod, Leonard demanded that neither Harris nor any priest ordained by her would be welcome to minister in the Church of England. McClean, who was piloting the legislation, did not see the necessity for such drastic action. After Runcie had taken advice from Habgood and others, senior officials were instructed to work into the early hours to produce a statement which made clear that Bishop Harris would not be permitted to carry out episcopal functions in the Church of England. The state-ment, read to the Synod by Runcie the following day, also made clear that no priest or deacon, male or female, ordained by her would be permitted to officiate in this country. The traditionalists saw the statement as winning another battle in the war.

Leonard's threat of schism was nevertheless echoed by, among others, Robinson in Sydney and handful of English bishops. But those most immediately affected were the dwindling band of American traditionalists, led by the aptly named Bishop Clarence Pope of Fort Worth, Texas. They called an international conference of sympathizers – soon dubbed the 'rebel Synod' – to be held in Fort Worth in June, and the fall-out of the Harris consecration made the prospect of a formal split in the American Church seem almost inevitable. While supporters of women priests celebrated, a tangible sense of crisis permeated the highest levels of the Church. It was felt not least by Archbishop Robin Eames of Armagh, the Primate of All Ireland, who had been appointed by Runcie to head the commission set up to extricate the worldwide Church from its predicament.

Eames and his seven-strong commission (which included the traditionalist David Hope, then Bishop of Wakefield) had until April – the date of the next meeting of the primates in Cyprus – to come up with a peace plan. The Lambeth Conference had recognized that there were two sides to the argument: Eames's job was to produce a formula which would allow both to live their separate lives under the same roof. A period of secretive shuttle diplomacy followed. The commission and Runcie held confidential talks with delegations of both liberal and traditionalist bishops in New York and London. The options under consideration ranged from the creation of a new, autonomous Anglican province for traditionalists – a parallel Church – to various versions of the 'episcopal visitors' scheme.

If the international scene was humming with behind-the-scenes activity, so was the national. The draft legislation, given its 'second reading' the previous year, was now at its 'committee' stage. The revision committee, chaired by the Bishop of Derby, the Rt. Revd Peter Dawes, had to examine more than 450 proposed amendments from a broad spectrum of Synod members. The 16-strong committee, augmented by the five members of the legislation's steering committee headed by David McClean, met privately seven times in 1989 in order to sift through the proposals and counter-proposals, often hearing the proposers put their case in person before deciding on the merits of the particular amendment by a vote. Most of the proposed changes were rejected, but fundamental alterations were agreed which had a profound impact on the character of the draft legislation.

The two key amendments were advanced in the revision committee by delegates from the House of Bishops. The House had decided the previous October, by a majority vote, that the safeguard allowing successive traditionalist bishops to declare a diocese a 'no go' zone for women priests was unacceptable because it would entrench schism permanently. They were prepared to put up with schism for an interim period in order to protect the consciences of the traditionalist minority already in the Church. But they were not prepared to split the Church indefinitely. Their first amendment, which was also backed by other Synod members, proposed that all the safeguards should have a 'sell by' date – 20 years – after which they would expire. Despite vigorous lobbying from the traditionalists, the revision committee accepted this time limit, with the slight modification that it could easily be extended by a simple majority vote in the General Synod.

The bishops' second amendment was equally contentious. It proposed that the draft legislation should be rewritten along the lines of the original House of Bishops' report, under which the safeguards would be available only to those bishops who were in office when the legislation was enacted. The traditionalists argued, forcefully, that such a move would ultimately drive them out of the Church. Any traditionalist clergyman offered the post of diocesan bishop once the legislation had been enacted could hardly square the job with his conscience because he would not enjoy the protection of the safeguards. If there were already women priests in the diocese to which he was being appointed, he would have no power to eject them. If there were not, he would have no power to prevent them being ordained if they were deemed worthy of ordination. He could (without fear of prosecution under the Sex Discrimination Act) refuse to ordain women himself and delegate the responsibility to a suffragan or assistant bishop who did not share his qualms. But this would not absolve him from responsibility; in theological terms, he would still be recognizing the validity of women as priests. A traditionalist of integrity would, therefore, be unable to accept the appointment. The knock-on effect would be devastating: middle-aged traditionalists could no longer hope for high office; young men would be deterred from training for the priesthood; eventually there would be no representatives of the traditionalist point of view among the diocesan bishops. After extensive debate, however, the amendment was accepted and incorporated into the draft legislation. While supporters of women priests were delighted to see the safeguards whittled down by the bishops and the revision committee, the traditionalists were seething. They knew, however, that they would have one last chance to influence the contents of the legislative package – at the November meeting of the General Synod.

At the end of April 1989, the worldwide Church's 27 primates – including Runcie, Browning, Tutu and Eames – gathered in a beach-side hotel in Larnaca, Cyprus, for the most important summit in the history of Anglicanism. On the eve of the five-day meeting, Runcie published a letter from the Pope which he felt illustrated Rome's continuing confusion about the structure of the Anglican Church. The letter was a thinly veiled appeal to Runcie to use his influence to prevent women being ordained priests in the Church of England. The Pope warned that relationships between the two leaders could become 'highly problematic' if the Archbishop's own province allowed the ordination of priests, regardless of the fact that they were already ordained elsewhere – a timely warning as Runcie was due to meet the Pope in Rome in September. But Runcie was taken aback by the letter because it demonstrated, once again, that Rome still believed the Church of England had a special significance in the Anglican Communion, even though unity talks had always been conducted at an international level involving all 27 Anglican provinces. The Pope's hint that constructive dialogue could only continue if the Church of England, Anglicanism's historic centre, rejected women priests, offended Runcie's sense of democracy. The Archbishop's response was immediate. He told his fellow primates that, at his meeting with the Pope, he would 'consciously represent' the whole Anglican Church and not just the Church of England. It was the kind of fundamental misunderstanding which had bedevilled the negotiations between the two churches from the outset, and it compounded Runcie's gloom about the possibility of ultimate success.

Internal Church unity was, however an even more pressing concern. In the air-conditioned cool of the hotel, the primates – many of whom had deep reservations about women priests – shut themselves away for two days of fierce debate before the final 25-page Eames report was issued on 29 April. It made clear that women bishops who were travelling in parts of the worldwide Anglican Church which did not accept them should conform to the local law. As a mechanism for allowing traditionalists and women priests to live side by side, the report endorsed the so-called 'episcopal visitors' scheme. But to the dismay, if not surprise, of the hard-line traditionalists, the report backed the 'watered down' version of the scheme already in use in the United States. Under this version, dissenting priests and congregations who found themselves in a diocese run by a woman bishop could place themselves in the care of a traditionalist bishop from another diocese. But such a transference of allegiance could only be made with the express permission of the woman bishop involved. For the traditionalists, this version of the scheme relied too heavily on the good will of the woman bishop, who could easily withhold her permission and leave the dissenters in her diocese stranded. They wanted written guarantees that would entrench the rights of traditionalists to receive episcopal care from a sympathetic bishop, regardless of the wishes of their own bishop. But the Eames report categorically rejected the idea that bishops with opposing views might operate in parallel in the same geographical areas. 'Parallel episcopal jurisdictions have the marks of schism,' it said. The report also developed the idea of reception, envisaging the remote possibility that women's ordination could be rejected after an unspecified trial period if found to be inconsistent with the 'mind of the Church'. But the development could also be overwhelmingly accepted as common practice. In the meantime, said the report, it would be wrong for traditionalist bishops to declare themselves out of communion with women bishops as a number, including Leonard, had already done. Communion may have been 'impaired' by the consecration of Barbara Harris, but it had not been broken.

The traditionalists' response was not long in coming. In the blazing Texas heat, 2,000 delegates – bishops, clergy and laity from all over the world – converged on Forth Worth just over a month later for what was, by any standards, an extraordinary event. Eight Church of England diocesan bishops and nearly a quarter of the membership of the General Synod signed a message of support, and Leonard attended in person. Few of the traditionalists had been impressed by the Eames report; plans to create a parallel 'Church within a Church' remained at the top of their agenda, and they rejected the idea that it would necessarily precipitate a schism. On the eve of the three-day 'rebel' synod, however, Runcie issued a heartfelt plea to the traditionalists, warning them that 'forms of separation' would not 'serve the cause of truth'.

The rebels were not in a listening mood. After an angry debate in which speaker after speaker ridiculed the liberals and accused the Episcopal Church of persecuting opponents of women priests, they voted to set up a parallel Church. A constitution was adopted and delegates agreed to establish a new structure of traditionalist dioceses and parishes entitled the 'Episcopal Synod of America'. They then went further by adopting the 'hard line' version of the episcopal visitors scheme which had been ruled out by the Eames commission. The traditionalist bishops vowed that they were ready to minister to like-minded congregations even if the relevant diocesan bishop objected. 'If we are cut off from our right to minister to the people, we have no future,' said one. At the same time, however, the leaders of the new grouping were adamant that it conformed to the laws of the Church, and was not schismatic. They were determined not to be the ones seen to initiate a split in the Church. Pope, the president of the 'rebel' synod, said in a letter to Runcie that 'by God's grace, we have been saved rancour, conflict and despair.' At the same time, however, he made the prospect of a schism appear almost inevitable by issuing a firm warning that any attempt to curtail the new organization's activities would be regarded as highly provocative. In a clear challenge to Browning, Pope vowed that the new body would not back down if national or regional Church authorities tried to interfere with it. In fact, the rebellion was short lived. In September, at a week-long summit in Philadelphia of the American House of Bishops, a body which now included Barbara Harris, a deal was struck. Pope and the other American traditionalist bishops, who had been in such belligerent mood only months before, agreed to respect the diocesan boundaries of their colleagues in return for a clear declaration by the liberals that they would respect the wishes of traditionalist congregations (a solution which was in line with the Eames recommendations). It appeared to be a grave setback for the international traditionalist movement; many had wanted Pope to waste no time in challenging the existing liberal establishment. He was accused of negotiating the deal – which few thought would stick – behind the backs of other traditionalists. In fact, the American traditionalist bishops were already working on far more radical plans. The cease-fire was a minor triumph for the conciliation skills of the Eames commission, which like an ecclesiastical United Nations, stepped in to monitor the uneasy peace that followed.

10

Crossroads

(1989–91)

Runcie's five-day visit to Pope John Paul II in Rome at the end of September was a high profile affair, but produced little of substance. The joint declaration signed by the two religious leaders formally recommitted them to search for unity. But it also recognized that the question of women priests was an effective bar to reconciliation. Nor was there any sign that Rome might be on the point of recognizing Anglican orders as valid. And another of Runcie's hopes for the trip – to try to hurry the Vatican into giving its long-delayed response to the ARCIC report in order to reinvigorate the unity negotiations – also proved frustrating; it was to be several more months before it emerged. Few suspected that the reason for the delay (the report had been decisively endorsed by the Lambeth Conference 18 months previously) was anything more sinister that Vatican red-tape. In fact, the Vatican was on the point of rejecting the report on which so many hopes rested, criticizing its methodology and demanding further clarifications. It was to prove another severe setback to unity hopes. Though he did not show it, Runcie was becoming increasingly despondent.

'We haven't had much movement in real terms on the Roman Catholic side,' he now argues.

> I still believe in the possibility of union but I don't believe it is on the immediate agenda. As far as I am concerned, we Anglicans belong to a body that has split off from Rome and I would be happy if Rome was able to absorb us back. But if

Rome seems unresponsive to what seems to me to be a development in the tradition, it is an added obstacle. But it may be an added obstacle to us to belong to a Church which these days is in danger of having, in the eyes of the world and a great number of Christians, the character of a male Mediterranean club. We are not ordaining women just to be devils. We feel compelled to do it because we think the point has arrived when there must be a question mark over our capacity to minster authentically to people in an incarnational way when the whole landscape of gender has changed.

On the other hand, he remains convinced that the pursuit of the grail of unity was justified, whatever stuttering it caused over women priests:

If we had pushed on with the ordination of women in the early eighties and not heeded the ecumenical argument, we would have more seriously undermined our relations with the Orthodox and Roman Catholic Churches. We would also have created many difficulties internally, we should have lost more people. I usually say that if we had the ordination of women in the beginning of the eighties, we would have lost 1,000 clergy. We will lose many fewer now.

The declaration may have appeared anodyne, but it stirred the embers. Its admission that women priests were a barrier to unity – hardly a novel sentiment but controversial because of its timing – was seized on with glee by the traditionalists. Implicitly, it once again raised the question of authority: could the Church of England, which claims to be part of the wider Catholic Church, make a decision about women priests independently of the Roman Catholic and Orthodox Churches? Surely the unity of Christendom – which was, after all, an explicit scriptural exhortation – must come before women's ordination in the order of priorities? Because he had handed such a propaganda coup to their opponents, the hapless Runcie was subsequently accused by the pro-women-priest camp of selling the women already ordained in other parts of the

Anglican Church 'down the Tiber'. The traditionalists were accused of attempting to polarize the argument, of suggesting the choice was either unity or women priests. But surely, member of MOW argued, the best way forward was to pursue both aims, particularly if the Roman Catholics could be convinced that the ordination of women was a valid development?

With so much depending on the November General Synod for both sides, the run-up to the debate was bound to take on the trappings of a show-down. More than a 1,000 black-cassocked traditionalist clergy gathered on 31 October at Church House for an extraordinary rally. Organized by the Anglo-Catholic Cost of Conscience movement as a show of strength, it became a call to arms. The military analogies were not lost on Leonard, who consolidated his standing as undisputed commander of the diehard faction by urging his troops to 'repel' the 'invasion' of women priests. 'At the same time, we must prepare for a possible continued existence in what would be occupied territory,' he told them to cheers. 'Blind resistance alone will not suffice, nor will preparation for the future alone suffice, for that implies that defeat is inevitable. We need both.' They gave him a standing ovation, and a fighting fund of £40,000 was rapidly collected. Resolutions attacking the draft legislation were passed overwhelmingly and hints were dropped that the traditionalists were prepared to go it alone and form an unofficial parallel Church which could sustain guerrilla warfare against the official Church for years to come if women were ordained. There was talk of legal actions and 'lock outs' – parishes barring their doors to their bishop. Plans were drawn up to create pockets of 'no-go' areas for women priests or any bishop who had become 'tainted' by ordaining them. These 'sterile' areas would be open to traditionalist bishops only. Over the coming months, four further rallies would be held – in Southwark, Manchester, Bristol and York.

An embattled air pervaded the General Synod when it gathered in Church House on 6 November to finalize the shape of the draft legislation. Supporters of women priests, who packed the public gallery, had earlier made their presence felt by staging a 24-hour vigil outside the gates of Lambeth Palace. The traditionalists indicated that they wanted major amendments made to the Measure to allow them to establish a parallel Church. As part of their tactics, they revived the radical notion of splitting the church into two self-contained parts; this was intended to act as a 'stalking horse' for the more pragmatic solution of 'non-territorial' dioceses, which could cater for traditionalist parishes which had 'opted out' of their own dioceses. Many on both sides of the debate felt that, in the jittery atmosphere of the General Synod, the success of the Measure was by no means a foregone conclusion; a negative speech by Runcie, for example, could still have torpedoed the whole project.

In the event, however, Runcie, albeit reluctantly, threw his weight behind the legislation, and it sailed through with a larger than expected margin. After a tense, uncomfortable debate – which included a dramatic resignation threat by the Bishop of Portsmouth, Timothy Bavin, and a typically rumbustious speech by David Jenkins – the Measure was approved by a simple majority in all three Houses. Runcie called for courage, but conceded he yearned for greater consensus; Bavin called for more time and said the legislation would undermine the role of the bishop as a focus of unity, making his position 'intolerable'; Jenkins said that the consciences of the opponents should be given no more considera-tion than those of would-be women priests. In the critical vote on the first clause, the bishops voted 30 to 17 in favour, the clergy 149 to 85 and the laity 144 to 78. It was a handsome majority, if still insufficient to give supporters confidence that it would achieve the two-thirds required at the final approval stage.

The traditionalists' amendments got nowhere. They lost all their battles but one: the proposed 20-year time limit on safeguards was dropped. Even supporters of woman priests felt that this was a somewhat arbitrary cut-off point; after all, how do you determine a date by when God is supposed to have made up his mind about the ordination of women? Crucially, however, the traditionalists failed to expunge the amendment which restricted to bishops in office the right to bar women priests from their dioceses. That remained at the heart of the legislation and was to prove a serious sticking point in the future. The separate, but linked, financial compensation

Measure was easily passed at the February General Synod. McClean attempted to play down fears of mass defections of clergy that would cost the Church millions of pounds in compensation. He predicted that, at the end of the day, fewer than 200 traditionalists clergy would resign, a very containable number. But the Bishop of Winchester, Colin James, a senior opponent of women priests, warned there could be many more refugees unless his liberal colleagues displayed more understanding of the predicament in which his fellow traditionalists found themselves. Too many of them were being told to lie down quietly or quit, he said. But they were a 'very precious element of the Anglican tradition' and should be safeguarded. Over the coming months and years, however, they were to feel increasingly persecuted.

Now that the General Synod – the apex of the Churches' hierarchical pyramid – had finalized the shape of the legislative package it was up to the dioceses, deaneries and parishes – the base – to pass their judgement. The 18-month-long consultation exercise was one of the widest in the Church of England's history. All 44 dioceses were required to debate and vote on the Measure; only if it was passed by a majority of diocesan synods could it proceed to its final approval stage in the General Synod; only if it received the necessary two-thirds majority there could it be referred to Parliament and, ultimately, Royal Assent. Surveys showed that the level of acceptance of the idea of women priests in the shires was high. In many areas, women deacons were already running strings of parishes, and some dioceses had appointed them to key posts such as rural dean, who is responsible for the welfare of dozens of priests. The General Synod, though it refused to sanction women deacons being given the title of team vicar, officially approved of their appointment as rural deans and residentiary canons (senior members of the staff at cathedrals) in November 1990. These were not the feminist, banner-waving, shock troops of the women's movement; they were brisk and efficient and low profile. A psychological study conducted by an academic at a Welsh university confirmed the widely-held view that the characteristics of male and female clergy were a mirror image of the rest of society: while the men exhibited feminine personality traits such as shyness and compassion, the women displayed a surprisingly masculine side, extrovert and less neurotic. In the battle to win hearts and minds in the pews these were important considerations. Esoteric concerns such as the ARCIC talks were largely lost on the average church-goer in a 'middle stump' middle England parish; they were more worried about the impoverishment of their Church which had resulted from the steep drop in the numbers of people coming forward for training as clergy. Even though, in the late 1980s and early 1990s, the numbers recommended for training evened out at about 430 a year, clergy deaths and retirements were outweighing ordinations. In many areas, a single priest had to look after four or five parishes, whizzing between them on a Sunday in a battered old car. Many parishioners, particularly in the shires, thought that if they gave the green light for women priests, the new injection of clergy would restore their cherished parishes to former glories. As much as anything, it was the manpower crisis within the Church of England which was forcing it to turn to women for its salvation.

With the disappearance of the legislation from the national arena the focus once again moved away from England, this time only as far as the other side of the Irish sea. The tiny Church of Ireland – of its 450,000 members, three-quarters live in the north – had at last reached its point of decision having, the previous year, approved the ordination of women in principle. A disestablished, low church, it had in the past been resented as the last remnant of the British Crown (despite its mediation work in Northern Ireland) but it now suddenly joined the vanguard of Ireland's nascent women's libera-tion movement. There was considerable resistance to women priests – partly because of the potential damage to relations with the numerically superior Roman Catholics, partly because of the lack of any real safeguards for Anglican dissidents. But Robin Eames, Archbishop of Armagh, and most of the bishops were in favour. On 15 May, after a good-humoured debate in a hall in Dublin, the Church of Ireland's General Synod voted by a narrow margin to ordain women; the decision, which needed a two-thirds majority, scraped through by four votes in the House of Clergy. A relieved Eames said the Church of Ireland had taken 'a step into the unknown'. A month later, it became the first part of the United

Kingdom – and the seventh Anglican province after the USA, Canada, New Zealand, Brazil, Kenya and Uganda – to ordain women. Kathleen Young, a widow trained as a physiotherapist, and Irene Templeton, mother of a boy aged five, were among six deacons ordained as priests at St Anne's cathedral, Belfast. Ructions followed; the traditionalists formed a breakaway faction called the Church of Ireland (Traditional Rite), which allied itself with the American-based continuing Church, the Traditional Anglican Communion, whose bishops had broken off all links with the Archbishop of Canterbury. 'We will not allow priestesses, liberalism and 'mother theology' to creep into our Church,' said a spokesman for the group. In terms of numbers, however, the breakaway body was tiny. The Church of England tried very hard to ignore the antics across the Irish sea. But the geographical proximity of women priests was a potent symbol of the advancing tide.

In his capacity as an ecclesiastical trouble-shooter, Eames had already spent much of the year embroiled in the issue of women in the Church. Penelope Jamieson, vicar of Karori West and Makara in New Zealand, had been elected to be bishop of Dunedin, making her Anglicanism's first diocesan bishop (Barbara Harris was an assistant bishop). She was an unlikely revolutionary; born in the Home Counties – Chalfont St Peter, Buckinghamshire – and educated at Edinburgh University, she had married a New Zealander and had lived there for 25 years. On a deliberately low-key visit to relatives in England in May she struck a conciliatory note. She said she knew of no opposition to her appointment in Dunedin, but if she encountered any pockets of resistance, she would deputize a male bishop to minister to the dissenters. The decision of the Anglican Church in New Zealand to be the first to consecrate a woman diocesan bishop was not unexpected – despite its air of Edwardian charm, it has always been radical, particularly in promoting Maori and women's rights – and has been at pains to emphasize its independence from the mother Church of England. At the consecration service in Dunedin on 29 July 1991, Jamieson and Harris, who was taking part, lit a miner's lamp which was brought back to England by a member of MOW as a symbol of the struggle. Ironically, the one New Zealand Anglican bishop to boycott the service was a Maori; he said his people were not ready to accept a woman as a bishop.

The Eames commission on women bishops, which had convened in March for its fourth meeting with the issue of women diocesan bishops high on the agenda, issued a further report at the end of April. It recognized that in certain parts of the Church, most notably America, the vital trust between traditionalist and liberal bishops was breaking down. In its report, the commission gave the primates of each province ultimate authority in cases of disputes; they were urged to ensure that dissenting parishes were provided with episcopal oversight, even to the point of overriding a diocesan bishop. The Eames ruling, however, kept power firmly in the hands of the liberal-dominated heirarchies. But the American traditionalists, led by Pope and backed by Leonard, were not satisfied; they wanted their own show. After consulting widely, the Episcopal Synod of America, the body set up at the 'rebel' Fort Worth synod, drew up a radical blueprint which, had it been adopted, would have provided the traditionalists with a secure future. It envisaged the creation of a new, 'shadow' province which, like the English traditionalists' 'non-geographical' diocese, would cater for dissenting parishes from across America – and ultimately from across the Anglican world. Far from being a temporary affair, the province, which would be officially recognized, would set up new parishes, train its own clergy and ensure a succession of bishops. A conference of 30 traditionalist bishops, including six English diocesans, met privately in London in May 1991 to press the case for such a worldwide network. This new group, which called itself the International Bishops' Conference on Faith and Order, called on 'all who feel alienated' to form 'separate Churches to work together with us . . . in communion with the See of Canterbury'. The group hinted that if its proposals were blocked, it might anyway form a semi-official network at odds with the mainstream Church. The proposals had to be taken seriously – they had heavyweight backing. But they were anathema to most of the primates. They would drive a coach and horses through Eames's ban on parallel Churches, and ultimately they fell on stony ground. The momentum generated at the Fort Worth Synod was fading away.

By the summer of 1990, the Church of England had reached a crossroads: two contests were underway which would shape its future. The first, the five-yearly elections for seats on the General Synod, involved much of the unseemly propaganda, underhand tactics and recriminations of secular political campaigns. Both sides knew that the legislation needed a two-thirds majority to succeed at its final approval stage in 1992, something it had never achieved. The pro-women's ordination camp was well aware that it had to pack the Synod benches with its supporters; the antis, meanwhile, pulled out all the stops to prevent them. Up for grabs were 183 seats in the House of Clergy (contested by 1,500 candidates) and 246 seats in the House of Laity (the House of Bishops has mainly an *ex officio* membership for the diocesan bishops with an extra nine places for elected suffragan bishops). Although ballot papers did not have to be returned to the dioceses until 4 October, the starting gun for campaigning had been fired as early as January when the Anglo-Catholic Church Union held the first of a series of training days for its candidates. Each place on the General Synod was contested by three to four candidates in what was often a bitter fight. Church in Danger, a group of Parliamentarians opposed to ecclesiastical liberalism, said in a letter to the *Church Times* (signed by, among others, John Gummer and three peers, that the choice for the electorate was between preserving the Church faithfully or accelerating its demise into a 'sectarian, exclusivist' body 'happy to see those who dissent and who have supported it through their lives become churchless or driven elsewhere'. Meanwhile, MOW bombarded the electors with leaflets, and even utilized the skills of the professional persuaders. A leading London-based advertising agency, GGK, whose clients included IBM and Swissair, agreed to give its services free, and designed inserts for MOW which were carried by the *Church Times* and the *Church of England Newspaper* (combined circulation, 60,000). Under the headline 'Will our Church be safe in their hands?', the advertizing depicted a woman administering the chalice and performing a marriage and a baptism. It read: 'In our Church women perform marriages, baptize and officiate at funerals. They wear clerical collars. They look like priests. They are trained as priests. Yet there is still resistance to the ordination of women.' When the results of the election were analysed in October, all that was clear was that a new bout of infighting lay ahead: the indications were that there had been a significant, but not decisive, shift in favour of the pro-women camp. The familiarity of the sight of women in clerical collars and the split in Anglo-Catholic ranks between the traditionalist and liberal (Affirming Catholicism) wings had contributed to the swing. There were 25 deacons elected to the House of Clergy and half the new lay members were women. The leadership of the Catholic group in Synod had been decimated by the deaths of Gareth Bennett and Margaret Hewitt, and the resignations or retirements of such leading figures as Oswald Clark and Brian Brindley. A two-thirds majority now looked attainable in both the House of Bishops and the normally obdurate House of Clergy. But the House of Laity was delicately poised. The outcome of the final approval debate remained tantalizingly close.

The second contest, though less open, attracted far more public interest and even took on the trappings of a national sport. A weary Runcie had announced in March that he was stepping down as Archbishop of Canterbury – the prestigious Lambeth stakes were underway. The summer buzzed with speculation. At one stage William Hill, the bookmakers, briefly suspended betting on the outcome after a suspiciously large amount was put on one bishop, suggesting insider knowledge. The mood had swung against the liberal camp (effectively ruling out Habgood) in favour of the Evangelicals: people were looking for an Archbishop who voiced certainties not subtleties. But there were few obvious candidates. In the event, the Crown Appointments' Commission and Mrs Thatcher (advised by three staunch Evangelicals - Prof Brian Griffiths, Head of her Policy Unit, Michael Alison, MP for Selby and Second Church Estates Commissioner, her former PPS and Robin Catford, the Prime Minister's Appointments Secretary) was unexpectedly speedy in arriving at a decision: George Carey, the Bishop of Bath and Wells. He may have been an outsider, but he had a seemingly pedigree track record – a relatively youthful Evangelical with a liberal tinge who would brook no nonsense from bishops who denied the reality of the resurrection but who was an uncompromising advocate of women priests. His appointment chimed well with the 'classless society' ushered in by the new Prime Minister, John Major. A workaholic from a working class background, Carey's seriousness contrasted with Runcie's light touch. What he lacked in finesse, however, he made up for in energy and a determination to lead from the front. But his initial tendency to charge at fences, however, caused more than a few palpitations at Lambeth Palace.

The traditionalists felt mixed emotions about his appointment. While they welcomed his doctrinal orthodoxy, they were under no illusions about his stance on women priests. Geldard recalls clashing swords with him over the issue in February 1983, when Carey was the principal of Trinity theological college in Bristol.

The city deanery of Bristol held a debate in a very Evangelical parish called Pip and Jim (St Philip and St James). The very dynamic Evangelical vicar and I spoke against Carey and someone else. In the debate we held our own, but it was very interesting that, in the pub afterwards, this vicar was very scathing about Carey, saying he wasn't a true Evangelical and had deserted the cause and all that.

Carey himself feels that though his background is Evangelical – he has experienced 'speaking in tongues' and has characterized Jesus as a 'management expert' who is 'looking for results' – he has since 'grown' into other traditions. But his unshakeable conviction that women should be priests has often shone through so sharply that his parallel ambition to unite the Church of England by reconciling the warring factions has been blunted.

Indeed, even before his enthronement in April 1991, the Archbishop-designate had thrown the caution of his advisers to the wind and blundered into a row which was to blight his future efforts at conciliation. In February, the *Reader's Digest* magazine published an interview with him which shocked even those who predicted he would be dogmatic on the issue of women priests. Asked why he felt so passionately on the issue, he replied: 'The idea that only a male can represent Christ at the altar is a most serious heresy. The implications of that are devastating and destructive, because it means that women feel excluded.' His use of the word 'heresy', the strongest insult one churchman can hurl at another, caused a furore. Kemp, in his capacity as the president of the Church Union, immediately called on Carey to withdraw his remarks. 'It is one thing to say that one's opponents are mistaken or in error,' fumed Kemp, 'but Dr Carey has taken a grave and inadmissible step in accusing them of a "most serious heresy." Carey, admitting he had 'put his foot in it', was forced into a rapid and damaging climb-down, explaining that he should have used the expression 'theological error'. But, in the eyes of many traditionalists, the stain was indelible.

Carey now explains:

The issue was not about the ordination of women to the priesthood. A lot of people misunderstood that. The issue was actually, who can represent Christ? Is it possible for women to represent Christ? I still hold to my view, because I believe that the whole point about Christology is that Christ became human; it wasn't that he became male. This concept of the male representing Christ is a mistake. My mistake, and I admit making this main mistake, was my dealing with a very complex issue in a journal such as the *Reader's Digest* which, in the circumstances of the interview, couldn't possibly cope with the intricacy of it.

Whatever Carey's rationale, however, the interview was a serious diplomatic gaffe. The damage could have been even more profound, however, if it had not been for the departure from the scene of potentially the greatest thorn in his flesh, Graham Leonard, who was 69. Leonard's announcement of his retirement as Bishop of London followed that of Runcie by several months, bringing to an end a fractious double act and a particularly turbulent era in the Church of England's history. It was a blow to the campaigners against women priests, particularly the diehards; they had lost an effective, if sometimes maverick, leader who was prepared to risk the hostility of his colleagues to voice unmalleable convictions. His successor, the Anglo-Catholic David Hope, was a more private individual who, while a vigorous and articulate opponent of women priests and the legislation, preferred to fight his battles behind closed doors. Hope, a bachelor with leanings towards monasticism, made it clear that he had no intention of leaving the Church of England if women were ordained, and at his appointment even MOW commented that he was unlikely to expend as much energy as his predecessor in battling with the pro-ordination lobby. Significantly, when the London diocesan synod came to vote on the legislation (which it opposed by a heavy majority) Hope upset some of the hard-line traditionalists by choosing the diplomatic course and abstaining. His relations with Carey, though often strained, were never as tempestuous as those of his predecessor. For one thing, Hope had a long-standing personal link with Carey which provided the two men with a better channel of communication: both were members of the same 'cell', one of the numerous small groups of priests who regularly share retreats and spiritual refresher courses. For another, Hope was a member of the Eames commission on women bishops (though he had also been a participant in the traditionalist International Bishops' Conference on Faith and Order). He was to be a key player in the coming months as the English hierarchy struggled to devise a formula to avert the catastrophe of schism. But in contrast to Leonard, he was to prove a team player.

11

Decisions and Divisions
(1991–93)

If the traditionalists – or at least the diehard tendency – were suddenly bereft of a natural leader among the bishops, there were clergy ready to step into the breach. George Austin, increasingly disillusioned with the Church's stance on issues ranging from homosexual clergy to feminist worship, led the charge. In a provocative sermon delivered from the pulpit of York Minster in September 1991, he repeated his call for the formal division of the Church of England into liberal and traditionalist wings. Such a partition was needed because the gulf between the two were 'now so great that they cannot continue to worship together,' he declared. The issue of women priests was ushering in a raft of liberal reforms which would destroy the traditional foundations of the Church. The hierarchy's response was sharp; Habgood, Austin's immediate superior, humorously likened him to the Fat Boy in the *Pickwick Papers* 'who creeps up on a timid old lady saying: "I want to make your flesh creep"'. Carey – whom Austin had only recently quizzically confronted in a corridor of Church House over his loose usage of the word 'heresy' – condemned Austin for indulging in the 'cavalier' language of Humpty Dumpty in *Alice in Wonderland*.

'I decided that people weren't hearing what was actually going on in the Church,' recalls Austin.

There was a big hidden agenda and supporters of women priests were being used. This issue was the tip of an iceberg and it would change the orthodoxy of the Church. So when I got permission to preach in the Minster, it just seemed I had to say the things I did. There were a few intakes of breath in the congregation. One man came round and said it was the most disgraceful thing he had ever heard and there was a coolness in the vestry from the canons. But apart from that the lay staff were very much with me. When I got home, there was a request to go to Bishopthorpe, Habgood's palace. I rang the secretary and asked whether I needed to wear an exercise book down my trousers, and she said she didn't think so. I confess it felt rather like an occasion at infant school when I had to go and see the headmistress for writing in chalk on the cardigan of the little girl in front. But he was alright. He didn't agree with my analysis. He said these things were not connected. But we agreed to disagree. Then Carey followed up with Humpty Dumpty, and nothing could have worked more in my favour.

Although another maverick, Austin – like Garry Bennett before him – echoed the gloom of a constituency which felt almost wilfully misunderstood. A trickle of Anglo-Catholic clergy were already leaving the Church of England for Rome – a prominent defector was Father Denys Lloyd, the principal of the Anglo-Catholic College of the Resurrection at Mirfield, south Yorkshire. Feminist theology seemed to be making inroads: a clergyman had caused uproar by referring to God as 'Herself' during prayers at the January General Synod, and a leading religious publisher produced a feminist guide to the Bible which cast Eve as an heroic figure. In America, a bishop had ordained a practising lesbian as a priest. The Church's prayer books were increasingly written in non-sexist 'inclusive' language, forcing out the richer but politically incorrect vocabulary of the past and subtly changing its meaning. The traditionalists felt that their whole world was slipping away. They were increasingly convinced that, by ordaining women priests, the Church was rejecting the way God created the world. Once the distinction between male and female had been discarded, there was no basis on which to challenge other aspects of the liberal 'hidden agenda'. Ironically it was Habgood, the target of Anglo-Catholic wrath in the wake of the Crockfords affair, who was now to prove the traditionalists' friend. In the coming months, as Carey became a distrusted figure, he was to assume a central role in the efforts to hold the Church together. Carey remains adamant, however, that his motives have been misinterpreted and that the view that he is the hawk and Habgood the dove is distorted. 'When I came to this office, I came with clear goals, and it seemed to me that we must deal somehow with the ordination of women to the priesthood,' he says. 'But I didn't come with a tough, uncompromising line. I came with the clear intention that somehow we must handle this in a proper and compassionate way.'

At the November 1991 General Synod, Carey's first as Archbishop of Canterbury, he warned that the Church of England was in danger of tearing itself apart over women priests and sought to appease his critics by calling on both leaders and members of the Church to show 'sensitivity and courtesy' to one another, a plea which provoked hollow laughter among the traditionalists. No one, Carey continued, should be making reckless prophecies about what might be the effect on the Church once the ordination of women was rejected or accepted next year. But both sides of the debate were furiously preparing the ground in case the vote went against them while simultaneously dismissing the other side's claims as scaremongering. Documents circulated at the Synod by Cost of Conscience, whose membership by then exceeded 3,000 clergy, explained the movement's detailed contingency plans (drawn up with legal advice) for a traditionalist parallel Church within the Church if women were ordained. The proposals envisaged the establishment of an alternative General Synod and network of traditionalist bishops designed to 'cocoon' traditionalist clergy and laity from contact with diocesan bishops who ordained, or even condoned, women priests. Traditionalist congregations which had declared themselves members of the network would remain legally under the authority of their diocesan bishop but, for all practical purposes, they would bypass him, calling on a traditionalist bishop from another diocese, or even another part of the worldwide Church, to carry out confirmations and other sacramental acts. If the diocesan bishop wished to challenge the right of the traditionalist bishop to trespass in his diocese without permission, he would be forced to apply to the courts. Cost of Conscience was confident that it would have a powerful legal argument in such a test case, namely that the Church of England had no authority to ordain women priests and that therefore the traditionalists represented the true Church of England. Traditionalist parishes might divert cash raised in the collection plate from their dioceses (all parishes are expected to contribute an annual 'quota' to central funds) to this new body, a serious threat to a Church under increasing financial pressure. But like all such proposals to split the Church into two, this scheme was greeted with derision by the majority of bishops. The pro-ordination camp was anyway unconvinced that many traditionalists would have the nerve to set up their own parallel Church, or leave for Rome, when the crunch came; they suspected that much of Cost of Conscience's support was 'soft' and was made up of moderate traditionalists whose main aim was to frighten the bishops into making further concessions. In addition, it was far from clear that Cost of Conscience's plan was legally watertight. Once the legislation had gained Royal Assent, the overwhelming probability was that the courts would rule that it represented the true mind of the Church.

Meanwhile, advocates of the ordination of women were becoming increasingly infuriated by the stalemate. They were particularly enraged by the notion held by some traditionalists that bishops who ordained women became 'tainted', a view they denounced as 'sexist voodoo'. As their anxiety grew about the outcome of the vote, they warned of the deep anger that would be unleashed on the Church if their will was frustrated at this late stage. With the draft legislation easily clearing the hurdle of the diocesan synods (38 of the 44 dioceses gave it the simple majority it required, though a third of the clergy who voted were against), they once again focused on the sophisticated electorate of the General Synod and, in anticipation of the Parliamentary battle ahead, on the House of Commons. The anti-ordination camp always had the ability to mobilize its allies in Westminster through groups like Church in Danger – in February, a Church in Danger open letter calling for a moratorium on the issue of women priests was signed by 36 peers and MPs, including two Ministers – and MOW now took steps to organize its Parliamentary lobby. A group of MOW clergy were able to counter Cost of Conscience: if the General Synod turned down the legislation, they would, they said, put a Bill before Parliament which would force the Church of England to ordain women. Emma Nicholson, a Methodist who was both a former vice-chairman of the Tory party and a newly elected MOW vice-moderator, agreed to sponsor what would be a Private Member's Bill. It was an ingenious notion and put the wind up the opposition, but the chances of a Private Member's Bill getting through the Commons if the General Synod had voted against the legislation were, in fact, negligible.

In January 1992, the legislation was thrown firmly back into the laps of the bishops. For many of them, it came as something of a shock and engendered a new mood of realism. Before the legislation had been sent to the dioceses, they could shy away from its practical ramifications. Suddenly, however, it was no longer an abstraction; the strong possibility was that the small print, which endorsed schism and virtually guaranteed open warfare, could soon be enshrined in the law of the land. Traditionalists would be driven out of the Church, form 'no go' ghettos or lock their doors to liberal bishops; legally ordained women priests would find themselves barred from large tracts of the country, calling into doubt their status and equality with their male counterparts. A ripple of panic spread through the episcopal ranks as they realized they might soon have to preside over this administrative and emotional mess. Some wondered if they had manufactured a Frankenstein monster that would turn on its creators and devour them. A consensus emerged between bishops on both sides of the divide that, if they wished to preserve the Church of England more or less intact, a far-reaching damage limitation exercise would be essential which ever way the November vote went. They were to be bitterly divided, however, over how this exercise should be planned. The first attempt to explore the terrain on the other side of the November vote occurred in January, when a group of four of them – led by the pro-ordination Bishop of Ripon, David Young, and which included Hope – produced a substantive paper which attempted to square the circle by suggesting ways in which dissidents could be cared for without sacrificing the authority of the diocesan bishops. The paper, which caused a flurry of excitement when it was published in the *Church Times*, argued that the draft legislation's bias in favour of supporters of women priests would drive an important body of Anglicans out of the Church, destroying its much-vaunted comprehensiveness. In order to stem the exodus, the Ripon plan envisaged the creation of two-tier dioceses: diocesan bishops in favour of women priests would be obliged to appoint a traditionalist suffragan to minister to parishes opposed to them; traditionalist diocesan bishops would appoint a suffragan prepared to ordain women to the priesthood. This would appease both supporters and opponents, do away with the necessity for no-go dioceses and also make it possible to appoint future bishops who had doubts over women's ordination, thus overcoming one of the traditionalists' central objections to the legislation. It was also consistent with the philosophy of the Eames commission. And it avoided the confrontational approach of Cost of Conscience.

The publication of the 'Ripon report' contributed to mounting pressure on the House of Bishops to postpone any decisions on the legislation until it could be substantially amended. Some thought that the Ripon plan or an equivalent could be integrated relatively easily into the legislation in the form of a non-binding code of practice; others wanted the legislation to be entirely overhauled and redrafted, a procedure that would take years. For a time, the whole process appeared to be unravelling. The pro-ordination lobby was, understandably, furious that the agonies of the 1,200 women deacons yearning for priesthood might be prolonged.

In fact, despite pleas for delays from some of the traditionalists, the House of Bishops was never likely to postpone the final vote on the legislation. A weariness with the issue had set in; people wanted it decided one way or the other. The momentum of the Church's new drive for recruits – the loudly trumpeted 'decade of evangelism' which had been launched in 1990 – had been largely paralysed by the introspective wrangling over women priests. The image of the Church was also suffering: the Methodists had appointed their first woman chairman, the direct successor of Wesley and their equivalent to Archbishop of Canterbury; a Church of Scotland minister had been appointed by the Queen as the royal household's first female chaplain. Carey was not only determined to give a lead, but he was convinced that the ordination of women priests would give the decade, his prized project, a new confidence. The House, at a private meeting in late January, voted convincingly to send the legislation on its way. The Ripon paper, though not acted upon, nevertheless marked the beginning of a lengthy examination of options to create 'space' for dissidents which would only come into its own after the result of the November vote was known. It represented a recognition that the bare bones of the legislation were insufficient to protect the unity and comprehensiveness of the Church, and that the law needed fleshing out. It also established that the traditionalist bishops, under the leadership of Hope, might be prepared to do what Leonard would not – negotiate. In the overriding interests of unity, it seemed, they might be prepared to forgo their right to declare their dioceses no-go areas in return for a package of credible measures they could sell to their constituency, or a significant section of it. A number of the more liberal bishops fiercely objected to the granting of more concessions to the traditionalists; they felt the safeguards in the legislation were already too generous and represented a slap in the face of women who had battled against extreme prejudice for equal treatment. But the majority were keener to preserve the united front of the bishops and the comprehensiveness of the Church than protect the sensitivities of women priests. Crucially, Habgood took this middle line. With this new-found common cause, the House of Bishops was able, decisively, to reject the Cost of Conscience parallel Church proposal as 'unacceptable'.

Soon afterwards, a five-strong House of Bishops sub-committee, chaired by Habgood and again including Hope, started meeting secretly to work out the best way to limit the damage after the November vote and care for the losers, whichever side they were. Carey recalls:

We knew there was going to be a pastoral job to be done, whatever happened, so we said in the House of Bishops that we should have a pastoral group under the leadership of the

Archbishop of York. It was decided that one of the Archbishops should be on it, and it was felt that I was a new Archbishop coming in and Canterbury's load is by far the heavier, so it would make sense for York, with his experience and knowledge of the bishops, to head up this committee. It was a decision made by the House of Bishops and it was the right one.

The dire consequences of episcopal disunity were dramatically brought home in February 1992 when an undignified row erupted in Australia following an attempt by a liberal bishop to ordain women priests before the Australian General Synod had given the green light. Although the Australian Synod had voted in favour of women's ordination three times since it had approved the idea in principle in 1977, the necessary two-thirds majority had never been achieved. Frustrated with the inflexibility of the Synod's procedures, Owen Dowling, the liberal Bishop of Canberra and Goulburn, decided to act unilaterally and ordain 11 women deacons as Australia's first women priests. But his decision was challenged by traditionalist clergy, who served an injunction in the secular courts. Dowling won the first round: despite the heavyweight opposition of Robinson, the conservative Evangelical Archbishop of Sydney, who argued that bishops should wait until a national policy had been decided by the Synod later in the year, the Australian Supreme Court ruled that Dowling could proceed. But on the eve of the planned ordinations, that ruling was reversed on appeal by a higher court, pending a full hearing. Dowling, an unlikely rebel, was furious, attacking the use of the injunction as 'an intolerable intrusion' into Church affairs. A groundswell of public opinion gathered behind him, and support came from several other diocesan bishops who vowed to go ahead with ordinations of women priests whatever the Synod decided (the Synod was, in fact, finally to approve the ordination of women priests in November). On 2 February, when the 'Goulburn 11' were due to have been ordained, hundreds of angry clergy and feminist supporters picketed St Andrew's cathedral in Sydney and St Saviour's cathedral in Goulburn 100 miles away. Eleven blood-red roses were laid on the steps of St Andrew's and Robinson was heckled by protesters, who cried 'shame, shame'. They did not have long to wait; the following month Peter Carnley, the liberal Archbishop of Perth, decided to follow Dowling's lead and, after an injunction against him had failed, he ordained ten women as priests – Australia's first – in St George's cathedral, Perth.

The episode provided a fillip to the Church of England's pro-ordination lobby: campaigners could now claim that nearly half the world's Anglican provinces – 13 out of 30 – now ordained women priests, of whom there were 1,342 worldwide. But it appalled the traditionalists. To them, it demonstrated how the liberals were prepared to flout any convention to get their way. The precedent also concerned the Church of England's bishops. As in Australia, the cumbersome quasi-parliamentary procedures of the Church of England's General Synod had deeply frustrated the progressives. While there was less chance of an English diocesan bishop acting on his own to ordain women if the General Synod rejected the legislation, some feared the Australian example could be repeated in England. Certainly, a growing number of the bishops were increasingly fearful about how they could contain the tidal wave of fury that would well up if, as was widely expected, the legislation fell at the last fence in November. The voting figures from the House of Laity at the York General Synod in July reinforced the view that the legislation would fail by a few lay votes to reach the required two-thirds threshold. If so, the matter could not be realistically brought back to the General Synod for a decade. The pro-women priest camp left no one in any doubt about the devastation that would ensue: retired bishops would illegally ordain women deacons as priests; clergy supporters of female ordination would refuse to celebrate Communion; senior liberal Churchmen would resign; male deacons would refuse to go forward to the priesthood. More unpredictable was the reaction of women in the pews. Would they stop coming to church? Would the regiment of 'holy dusters' who daily burnished the country's 13,000 parish churches withdraw their labour? Bishops began drawing up contingency plans to cope with the emotional aftermath of the vote: dates were left free in diaries for meetings with distraught parishioners; professional counsellors were put on stand-by. In this vacuum of uncertainty, the Church seemed to have lost any sense of purpose.

With his leadership of the Church of England coming under increasing fire – senior churchmen of every shade were openly casting doubt on his judgement and sureness of touch – Carey travelled to Italy in May to meet a handful of senior Roman Catholic leaders. Though the highpoint of his trip was his first meeting with the Pope, he also stopped off in Milan where he spent some time with the liberal Cardinal Carlo Martini, the man tipped by many to be the next Pope. His talks with Martini, a Jesuit, proved more rewarding than those with John Paul II. In contrast to Runcie, who had made it clear that he believed the Pope to be the most important bishop in the universal Church, Carey regarded himself as having equal status as a fellow head of an international denomination, so he was determined not to appear deferential. The two held a 'gracious' conversation in the Pope's private study in the Vatican, but there was little meeting of minds over the issue of women priests. The visit merely confirmed the distance between the two Church leaders, but it was of little moment: for most Anglicans, the women's ordination issue had by now taken priority over reunion with Rome. As Austin puts it: 'Suddenly, it was like a submarine coming up through a trawler and the whole things sinks. And the awful thing is how no one seems to care.'

The summer of 1992 proved long and hot, in every sense. With only a few months to go before the decisive November vote, the pro- and anti-ordination lobbies went into overdrive to capture the handful of General Synod votes that would win or lose them the day. On 13 June, the traditionalists staged a vast, all-day rally in Wembley arena. Black-cassocked priests sweating under their birettas cooled off with ice creams as steel bands entertained the 6,000-strong crowd. John Gummer, the main speaker, was in tub-thumping form as he lacerated 1960s-style liberalism, called for a return of traditional Christian teachings and warned that the Church of England would disintegrate into a 'muddled sect' if women were ordained as priests. 'Archbishop,' he exhorted the absent Carey, 'you inherited the Church hesitant; make it again the Church militant.' More than 50 bishops – including Robinson from

Sydney and Pope from Fort Worth – were involved in the climax of the event, a Communion service celebrated jointly by 1,000 clergy; it took 15 minutes for them to file into the arena behind a priest swinging a censer. At the same time, at the other end of London, supporters of women priests were staging a smaller, if no less vociferous, gathering. At a service in Southwark cathedral to celebrate the fifth anniversary of the ordination of England's first women deacons, Harriet Harman, the Labour MP for Peckham, told the congregation: 'I've always said a woman's place is in the House. By that I mean the House of Commons, and we know that a woman's place is also in the House of Bishops.' There was no incense: instead, the women deacons processed to the altar to the strains of 'Freedom is Coming, Oh Yes I know'.

In the final weeks before the November vote, MOW made a well-timed late run. Effectively ignoring the appeals by the Archbishops of Canterbury and York for an end to campaigning and name-calling, five bishops (all closely linked with MOW) broke ranks in October to jointly sign a letter to all Synod members which urged them to pass the legislation. A few days later, MOW produced Virginia Bottomley, the Health Secretary, who declared her support for women priests at a press conference in the House of Commons – putting her at odds with her Cabinet colleague, John Gummer. MOW was on a roll, and the impetus was maintained with another slick advertizing campaign in the Church press. The bombardment of Synod members and bishops with letters and leaflets was stepped up. In retrospect, the traditionalist campaign had probably peaked at the General Synod in July, when they appeared to be on course to defeat the legislation. Some traditionalist leaders feel in retrospect that their most disastrous political misjudgement was to force a division of Houses at the York Synod. The tactic allowed the votes to be counted and analysed, but instead of reinforcing the traditionalists' position, it galvanized the pro-women camp. MOW's late surge took them into the lead just at the right time.

The aftermath of the 11 November final approval vote was traumatic. A strange pall of uncertainty hung over the Church. Many were worried or confused by what was happening, others were hopeful and waiting to be enthused. But, despite the fact that many of the bishops had come to believe that the ordination of women would be the Church's most inspiring act this century, their leadership had been inhibited by Carey's call for a 'period of reflection'. Instead of being able to march the Church into a new age, they were left countering the rearguard action being fought by the traditionalists. The official line was: wait, be patient and we will accommodate many of your concerns. Bishops up and down the country were holding private meetings with groups of distressed clergy, though some of the more liberal bishops made little effort to disguise their wish to see the diehards leave. Jenkins, for example, accused opponents of women priests of 'huffing and puffing' and wanting to create 'ghettos' based on fantasies of medieval Rome or Constantinople. Carey, who talked to a range of dissidents from Tony Higton, the conservative Evangelical Essex vicar, to Geoffrey Rowell, an Oxford theologian and former close ally of the late Garry Bennett, repeatedly sought to calm emotions by playing down claims of a mass exodus, stressing that everyone would be able to stay in the Church with honour. In fact he angered many traditionalists who felt he was belittling the strength of their feelings and the depth of their fears. Amid an atmosphere of paranoia, suspicion and distrust, they accused some of the liberal bishops of trying to force them out of the Church. If anything, their attitudes hardened. Having initially scattered like a retreating army, they regrouped under two main banners, those who were looking to Leonard to take them to Rome and those who were digging in for a bloody battle.

Leonard had begun holding private meetings at Archbishop's House with Cardinal Hume, with whom he developed a strong personal rapport, soon after the November vote. At later meetings (there were about half a dozen) he was accompanied by his lieutenants, Geldard and Canon Christopher Colven, master of the exclusive, 800-strong Society of the Holy Cross from whose ranks many of the converts would come. The 'Anglo-Papists', as some called them, were looking for a way to overcome Rome's official stance that the Anglican orders they were about to renounce were null and void; they were distressed by the idea that when they were reordained as Roman Catholic priests, they would have to concede that their lives up to that point had been a sham. Many of them, including Leonard, had ensured that Old Catholic bishops had participated in their ordinations as Anglican clergy to demonstrate their belief that they were part of the universal Catholic Church.

Leonard was also looking for some sort of arrangement which would give the converts a special status as a group; if normal procedure had been followed, they would have been required to convert individually in the local catechism classes run by parishes for all-comers. But not only did they feel that, as they were theologically literate, they should have a fast track into the Roman Catholic Church, they also wanted to preserve something of their Anglican ethos and liturgy when they got there. Many Anglo-Catholics were happy with the post-Vatican II modernization of Roman Catholic worship, but others looked askance at the proliferation of tambourines and guitars and wanted to retain the dignity of traditional Prayer-Book services. Leonard proposed two models: a personal prelature, in which the Anglican converts would come under the authority of a sympathetic prelate rather than their local Roman Catholic bishop, and a uniate Church, an independent body with its own practices and traditions which was nevertheless fully accepted by Rome. Both these models had precedents (though the main precedent for the former was the deeply unpopular ultra-traditionalist lay movement Opus Dei), but they were too radical for many Roman Catholics. The English hierarchy was particularly sensitive both to its future relations with the Church of England, which would deteriorate even further if it was thought to be trying to 'poach' large numbers of Anglican priests, and to the feelings of its own clergy. Some of the Roman Catholic bishops feared that there would be serious resentment among their own celibate priests, some of whom were anyway sympathetic to the idea of ordaining women, if they admitted a large group of married (or repressed homosexual) ultra-traditionalist former Anglicans to the priesthood and gave them special status and the right to use antiquarian forms of worship. Some of the bishops were anxious to set conditions which would weed out these extremists while ensuring that some of the brightest and best of the Anglo-Catholic clergy would feel welcome and valued. In America there existed a precedent, set in the 1970s, in which individual congregations had transferred to

Rome as a group, led by their clergy. A version of this model had many advantages; it operated on a smaller scale than that envisaged by Leonard, and it could allow converts, rather than remaining in their ghetto, to become fully integrated into the Roman Catholic Church.

Whatever the resistance from within his own ranks, Cardinal Hume was determined to do everything he could to ease the passage of disaffected Anglicans into his Church. He believed that an historic moment in the history of English Catholicism had arrived and had to be seized – the influx of the cream of Anglo-Catholicism could bring the Roman Catholic Church into the mainstream and result in the healthy recasting of English Christianity: a strengthened Catholic wing in the Roman Catholic Church and a renewed Protestant wing led by the Church of England. Hume's enthusiasm was largely shared by the Pope. At one meeting with the traditionalists in the library of Archbishop's House, Hume arrived late, having just been on the telephone to Rome. He had scribbled something on the back of an envelope and announced to the meeting that it was a message from the Pope who asked them, simply, to remember Acts 15, verse 28. There followed a pregnant pause because, despite the presence of a Cardinal, a handful of bishops and several senior clergy, no one could remember the biblical text the Pope was referring to. Then someone found a Bible and read the verse out: 'For it has seemed good to the Holy Spirit and to us to lay upon you no greater burden than these necessary things.' The quotation brought tears to their eyes.

Meanwhile, those traditionalists who elected to stay and fight pooled their resources and formed Forward in Faith, an umbrella organization for traditionalist pressure groups such as Cost of Conscience, Women Against the Ordination of Women and the Church Union which represented about 30,000 laity and (at its height) 6,500 clergy, some of whom were retired or from overseas. Some, like Austin, could hardly conceive of leaving the Church of England; others saw their rearguard action as offering breathing space before they, too, sought sanctuary in the Roman Catholic or Orthodox Churches. According to their own calculations, they were strongest on the ground in the West Country, the South East, particularly London, and the Midlands – in the Chichester diocese they had the support of 40 per cent of the clergy. They were prepared to use a range of weapons, from the law courts to the withholding of parish quotas, to consolidate their position. As they stepped up their demands for the creation of a 'Church within a Church', the critical question was whether they would receive the support of the traditionalist bishops, the 13 who voted against the legislation. Would these bishops use their rights under the legislation to declare their dioceses 'no-go' zones for women priests and, if necessary, precipitate schism by backing an unofficial traditionalist network?

Hope and his traditionalist colleagues had already secretly formed a group which met regularly at his London flat to discuss tactics (four or five archdeacons also attended the meetings). They were daily receiving dozens of anguished letters from traditionalists, often from clergy they had never realized shared their views. Hope, however, preferred compromise to confrontation. He and his fellow traditionalist bishops – the Bishop of Sheffield, David Lunn, (who had threatened to resign as a bishop during the November debate) and the Bishop of Sodor and Man, Noel Jones, were particularly outspoken – were determined to try to force concessions out of the House of Bishops, even if these concessions would not satisfy the diehards in Forward in Faith. Habgood's sub-committee, of which Hope was a member, was rapidly reconvened to work on damage limitation plans. The group was already thinking about drawing up options for pastoral provision, including some form of 'episcopal visitor' scheme. Carey and his senior colleagues were acutely aware of the dangers of dissenting parishes going down the Cost of Conscience road by inviting in traditionalist bishops from outside the Church of England hierarchy over the head of the diocesan bishop. Retired bishops, or bishops from aborad, would be loose canons; they would be outside the authority of the hierarchy and therefore schismatic.

Forward in Faith, meanwhile, had not given up hope of halting the legislation, though realistically there was only one hurdle left at which it might stumble – the parliamentary ecclesiastical committee. This obscure body – technically a select committee – consisted of 15 peers and 15 MPs, and its sole role was to vet

Church legislation before it could be debated on the floor of the Commons and the Lords. Like other select committees, it could attempt to tease out the nuances of the legislation by questioning officials, up to and including the Archbishop of Canterbury. The committee had no power to kill the legislation, but it could declare it 'inexpedient'. Such a ruling on the women priests legislation would have precipitated a constitutional crisis; the Church would have been forced either to amend the legislation and return it to the General Synod, a process that could take years, or bypass the committee and submit it directly to the Lords, an unprecedented step which risked incurring the wrath of Parliament. The traditionalists therefore rallied their forces in Parliament and were able to increase their representation on the committee. Indeed, the Whips who would normally have had some difficulty rounding up enough Parliamentarians to fill the seats suddenly found themselves inundated with requests to occupy the vacancies that became available after the 1992 general election. Nevertheless, the balance of the committee, which was chaired by Lord Templeman, the Law Lord, remained narrowly in favour of women priests. Advocates of women priests like Baroness Seear and Simon Hughes, the Liberal Democrat MP for Southwark, were in the majority; Anglo-Catholics such as Gummer and Patrick Cormack, Tory MP for Stafford, remained a vociferous minority. But speculation nevertheless grew that the committee might at least delay the legislation because of concern over the contentious clause 2 – which empowered bishops in office when the law was enacted, but not their successors, to bar women priests from the dioceses. Even those committee members who favoured women priests, including Frank Field, Labour MP for Birkenhead, were struck by the force of the traditionalists' argument that this provision would ultimately result in the withering away of the Anglo-Catholic wing of the Church. Privately, most traditionalists acknowledged that if the legislation surmounted this obstacle, the war was all but over. All the indications were that both the Lords and the Commons would give it their blessing. Parliament was, however, notoriously unpredictable and, psychologically, many could not finally resign themselves to defeat until the first women were ordained to the priesthood.

12

Departures
(1993–94)

In the middle of January 1993, the House of Bishops congregated in
Parker's hotel in Manchester for one of the most important meetings of its history. Its task was to hammer out a formula to stave off
the threatened schism, stem the impending exodus to Rome and
preserve unity. Morale was not high. Habgood's sub-committee
had distributed a paper containing the sketchy outlines of various
options, but for some of the liberal bishops even the most modest of
them – an informal scheme to allow neighbouring diocesan bishops
of opposing views help each other out – was a concession too far;
they felt they were being bullied into giving ground unnecessarily.
But the traditionalist bishops were pushing for the inclusion of a far
more ambitious option which was to become known as the 'flying
bishops' scheme. Under this arrangement, bishops who ordained
women would allow colleagues who did not (the so-called 'flying
bishops') 'landing rights' in their dioceses to minister to dissenting
parishes. These 'flying bishops' – the technical term was provincial
episcopal visitors – would be specifically appointed to this roving
role by the Archbishops of Canterbury and York. They would be
required in all cases to gain the permission of the diocesan bishop
before 'landing', but such permission could not be reasonably
refused.

The liberals recoiled at the idea of allowing these itinerant
bishops who did not recognize women priests into their dioceses.
But they were reassured by the promise that the provincial visitors
would have the status of mere suffragan (assistant) rather than

diocesan bishops, and would operate on a tight leash. Moreover –
despite pressure from the traditionalists for at least five roving
bishops – there would be a maximum of three of them, two in the
south of England (the province of Canterbury) and one in the north
(York). The 'flying bishops', the liberals hoped, would operate like
firemen, only called in an emergency. They were an 'extension' of
episcopal oversight rather than a parallel operation; in most cases,
diocesan bishops already planned to offer opponents of women
priests the services of a traditionalist suffragan bishop in the diocese
or would find an appropriate bishop in his region. But hardline
traditionalists did not like the idea of being ministered to by a
suffragan, however sympathetic, if he was merely acting on behalf
of an unsympathetic diocesan; to agree to this was playing along
with the 'deception' that women could be priests. Instead, they
wanted dissenting parishes to have the automatic right to call on the
services of their local 'flying bishop', whatever the wishes of the
diocesan.

The four-day residential conference lived up to the billing
supplied by one observer: episcopal poker. A few days before it met,
Forward in Faith raised the stakes by promising insurrection if its
demands were ignored. John Broadhurst, the pipe-smoking
London priest who chaired Forward in Faith and who had previously counselled caution, threatened to unleash the dogs of war.
'Until now we have been holding people back and telling them to act
with restraint. It only needs us now to say "go for the throat" and
the Church of England will break up,' he told a London meeting.
The threats only served to enrage the liberal bishops, who argued
fiercely in Manchester against making concessions. The atmosphere was, at times, belligerent, and the debate was fierce. The
Bishop of Leicester, Thomas Butler, was one of several forceful
opponents of the traditionalists' stance. But Habgood exerted pressure on all the bishops in the knowledge that the agreement of the
whole House was vital if a peace plan was to stick, and the key
moment occurred when the bishops decided they must remain
united. The three-page statement, hammered out over the last two
days of the meeting, was intended to contain the broad principles of
an agreement to be fleshed out later in the summer, but every word

counted. As they worked, they kept a wary eye on the faces of Kemp and Rogerson. These two represented the extremes; if they could live with the statement, everyone could. To general astonishment, the document – which envisaged the appointment of 'flying bishops' without spelling out their role – was agreed unanimously. The feeling of relief at the end of the meeting was palpable and many of the bishops wept openly. Others burst into song. 'I saw tears in many eyes other than my own,' said one. 'It was the sense that we had been drawn together in a brotherhood, which was historic and deeply moving.' Carey recalls: 'I remember feeling amazed that we were completely unanimous in our commitment to this document.'

The Manchester statement was a classic Anglican compromise, grounded in the laudable desire that the majority and the minority, the 'two integrities', should try to cohabit under the same roof, like a warring couple trying to save their marriage. But, based as it was on the bizarre idea of reception – that the only way to judge which of the two mutually exclusive positions was consistent with God's intentions was to wait and see which flourished and which withered away – it was deeply flawed. Like the White Queen in *Alice in Wonderland*, the bishops were prepared to believe two impossible things before breakfast to preserve the harmony of the Church of England. After all, many of them reasoned, the Church was no stranger to such untidiness; it had lived with such contradictions since its inception. But some of the proponents of female ordination felt it was ludicrous and offensive to speak of two integrities, even on an experimental basis, when the General Synod had clearly expressed its mind so clearly in November. To them, the bishops had gone too far in acknowledging the rights of the minority in order to preserve their own collegiality. Ironically, a similar stance was taken by hardline traditionalists, though for the opposite reasons. From their perspective, the statement failed to go far enough in keeping the 'two integrities' apart. Even more disturbing to the diehards was the fact that the traditionalist bishops to whom they looked for leadership had been prepared to sign up to the statement, apparently for the sake of peace and quiet within the House of Bishops. In public, Forward in Faith said the plan was a contribution to their aim, 'but it does not yet satisfy all our requirements.' In private, they began to accuse the traditionalist bishops of deserting them.

While the statement did much to reassure the broad Church that the bishops were genuinely attempting to hold the Church together, it did little to allay the suspicions of the traditionalists. As the bishops returned to their dioceses, they were surprised to be greeted by howls of outrage. One bishop received what he described as 'hysterical faxes' accusing him of betrayal; others found their post swelled with letters written in green ink. Noel Jones, a council member of Forward in Faith, received a mauling from his fellow council members when he briefed them about the statement, particularly when he made clear that the traditionalist bishops were standing firm with their colleagues in the House of Bishops. Austin, John Broadhurst and David Silk relayed their concerns to the two Archbishops at a meeting in Church House in February. It became rapidly apparent that the breakdown in trust between the hierarchy and the traditionalist constituency was more serious than originally thought; many blamed the level of venom and hate on Carey's often clumsy attempts to lead from the front. Increasingly, Habgood was left to pick up the pieces. The traditionalists were soon telling him that, as it stood, the Manchester statement was little more than a piece of paper which could be torn up at any time – the ecclesiastical equivalent of Neville Chamberlain's 'peace in our time' agreement on the eve of World War II. Ideally, they wanted the 'flying bishops' scheme incorporated into the legislation on women priests – or presented as a separate measure to Parliament – so that it would have the force of law. The 'flying bishops' would then become a permanent feature of the Church, providing the foundations, many still hoped, for some form of parallel Church. To demonstrate their unity of purpose, Forward in Faith organized a dramatic show of strength during the February General Synod. More than 100 traditionalists walked out of the Synod at a preordained moment to stage a 'rebel' Synod across the road in Methodist Central Hall. The meeting pointedly discussed setting up national structures which could form the skeleton of a parallel Church.

But it was clear that a growing number – about a third of the membership of Forward in Faith – was abandoning any hope of securing a niche in the new-look Church of England. For them, the promised land was Rome (though a number were attracted to Orthodoxy – 22 Anglican priests formed a group called Pilgrimage to Orthodoxy in June – and the 'continuing' Anglican Church). Carey had conceded, in a speech to Belgian Roman Catholics in February, that the 'dreams and visions' of reunion between the Churches had now 'faded into a mist of disappointment'. The prospect of capturing so many Anglican priests had turned the heads of many English Roman Catholics who felt they had in the past been treated as second-class citizens of dubious loyalty by the Church of England. This sense of euphoria even affected Hume who, in an unguarded moment, told the Roman Catholic weekly *The Tablet* in March that

> this could be the moment of grace, it could be the conversion of England, for which we have prayed all these years. I am terrified now we are going to turn round and say we do not want these newcomers. We have prayed for Christian unity and now it could be happening: a realignment of English Christianity so as to bring us together in two blocs, instead of two lots of blocs.

The triumphalist tone of the phrase 'the conversion of England' infuriated many Anglicans – who pointed out that there was two-way traffic between the Churches – and aroused the atavistic suspicions of conservative Evangelicals, for whom it summoned up images of the Armada and the Gunpowder Plot. Hume rapidly withdrew the phrase, but it was a revealing Freudian slip. He and many Roman Catholics certainly hoped that the injection of Anglican clergy would bolster the growing 'Englishness' of his Church, which had too often been regarded as little more than an extension of the diocese of Dublin. There was also much heady talk – fuelled by high-profile converts like Gummer and Widdecombe (who was received into the Roman Catholic Church in April) and the subsequent conversion of the Duchess of Kent – that the Roman Catholic Church would assume the mantle of the national church as the Church of England declined into a liberal Protestant sect. In fact the Roman Catholic Church was never on the verge of an instant breakthrough; if a realignment was underway it would take decades to become apparent.

In this atmosphere, however, the expectations of many of the Anglo-Papists were artificially high; they believed Hume was about to announce a detailed package to allow them to transfer their allegiance in groups and providing a 'fast track' for married and single Anglican clergy. In fact, the English Roman Catholic hierarchy could only move at the pace of Rome, and the sense of urgency among the key players in the Vatican – Cardinal Edward Cassidy, Willebrands's successor at the council for the Promotion of Christian Unity, and the ultra-orthodox Cardinal Joseph Ratzinger, head of the Congregation for the Doctrine of the Faith – hardly matched that felt in England. While many in Rome shared Hume's enthusiasm for seizing the moment, others were wary of allowing on board a group of ultra-traditionalist Anglicans who, they suspected, wanted a 'flag of convenience' for pursuing their own agenda. In early April the Vatican released a carefully-balanced statement – its first word on the subject. While giving its blessing to the negotiations between Hume and the traditionalists over the 'Roman option', it said that opposition to women priests was not in itself a qualification for conversion. Rome, it added, had no intention of poaching Anglican clergy, nor of upsetting ecumenical relations. Hume, who had himself held private meetings with both Carey and Hope, flew to Rome a few days later for further guidance. When the English Catholic hierarchy issued its initial statement on the issue after its four-day Low Week meeting at the end of April, it was disappointingly short on detail. To many it came as something of an anti-climax. The statement set out one crucial principle: that would-be converts could be received in groups under 'temporary pastoral provisions', but that, over time, they would be expected to become fully integrated into the Roman Catholic community – there was to be no permanent reserve for ex-Anglicans. The statement also agreed to the setting up of a joint Church of England/Roman Catholic commission to minimize friction between the Churches over the issue. Beyond that, there was very little. Forward in Faith welcomed the statement, saying that it would give hope and encouragement to 'many of our members who, since 11 November, have been confused, broken and on the verge of despair.' But over the coming months, many traditionalists would become increasingly frustrated with the inability of the English Roman Catholic bishops to extract final decisions from Rome. As one traditionalist put it later: 'The Catholic bishops missed a critical psychological moment. If they could have given a strong green light at that stage, thousands would have gone over.'

Meanwhile, within the Church of England, the fragile collegiality achieved by the House of Bishops in January was cracking up. The traditionalist group, led by Hope, were pushing for more concessions as they came under huge pressure from their constituency. Allegations flew around that a number of liberal bishops were turning away would-be ordinands who could not accept women priests, and rural deans and archdeacons were putting pressure on traditionalist clergy to quit. In May, Hope unveiled a radical blueprint for the diocese of London which his traditionalist colleagues hoped could be replicated up and down the country. His plan was, effectively, a modification of the parallel Church idea. But instead of a Church within a Church, he proposed to create a diocese within a diocese. At a press conference, Hope announced that, after months of 'anguish and prayerful consideration', he had decided to waive his right under the legislation to declare his diocese a 'no-go' zone for women priests and agreed that women could be ordained there, a disappointment if not a surprise to the traditionalists and a delight to the 60 or so women deacons in London. But Hope said that the women would be ordained neither by him nor by any of his area bishops acting on bis behalf. Instead, a bishop acting as a 'commissary' of the Archbishop of Canterbury would carry out the ordinations, putting Hope at arms length from the process and ensuring that neither he nor his area bishops were disowned by the traditionalist clergy and laity. In addition, the traditionalists in the diocese would be able to opt into their own, hermetically sealed enclave within the diocese – a non-geographical grouping of parishes that voluntarily put themselves under the jurisdiction of the traditionalist suffragan Bishop of Fulham.

The London plan was seen by the traditionalists as the best way to develop the January Manchester statement, and Kemp drew up a national scheme based upon it to present to the House of Bishops when it met in June to flesh out the statement. The traditionalists kept emphasizing that the liberals had agreed to accommodate the 'two integrities': now they must match their words with concrete proposals. But the supporters of women priests were becoming more determined to resist further concessions, and the tensions between the bishops burst into the open. Santer told a meeting in his diocese: 'Let me tell you that those traditionalists who are determined to stay and wreck the Church will find their souls in grave peril.' The Bishop of Oxford, Richard Harries, whose diocese contained a high concentration of Anglo-Catholic clergy, rejected the London plan, saying that the January statement could not be altered. Baker of Salisbury demanded a ban on the ordination of traditionalists who denied the possibility of women becoming priests. Jones denounced Baker's comments as 'offensive', adding: 'My blood pressure is up.' As the atmosphere soured, Carey seemed to many to be floundering. Again, the effective running of the Church appeared to pass, by default, to Habgood. Kemp said on a radio programme on Good Friday that Habgood had been working 'very hard' while the general perception was that Carey was doing 'far less'. As one traditionalist put it: 'Carey doesn't understand us, so he doesn't care about us.' In retrospect, Carey is sanguine:

> Well, I think someone has to be the villain. I think the price of leadership is sometimes misunderstanding. If you make a clear speech like I did in Synod people are going to say, 'well, he's got no time for us'. But the Archbishop of York was there to provide a safe pair of hands and to be there for those to whom the Archbishop of Canterbury appeared too hawkish. So I hope people will realize as time goes on that in fact it was team work – and that behind the scenes I was supporting bishops, working closely with the Bishop of London, providing, for instance, the necessary commissary for the London scheme to work. So the impression that I was less Catholic is just not correct.

But Carey – and those senior Church officials responsible for the legislation – nevertheless faced the uncomfortable prospect of a grilling from members of the Parliamentary ecclesiastical committee. The preliminary skirmish took place in a House of Commons committee room on 19 April 1993. In front of the television cameras, members of the Church of England's legislative committee – led by McClean and the Bishop of Guildford, Michael Adie – found themselves receiving an unexpectedly rough ride. The unease felt by many that Clause 2 of the legislation was inadequate to protect the traditionalist minority unless the January Manchester statement was significantly toughened up and given some force in law was powerfully expressed by Field and Cormack among others. Was the minority going to be dealt with tolerantly 'or is the Measure in effect a measure that Joe Stalin would be proud of because it is going to drive out over a period of time all those who are opposed?'was one of Field's stinging questions. Cormack pressed Adie: 'What do you think about the constitutional rights of those of Her Majesty's subjects who were baptized into the Church of England when women priests were not allowed, who had their children baptized into such a Church and who wish to be able to look for many generations hence to episcopal oversight in such a Church?' Cormack's remarks provoked an angry rebuke from another committee member, the liberal Baroness Seear, who reminded the committee of the 'rights and needs and anxieties and dreams and visions' of the would-be women priests. But even Simon Hughes and Stuart Randall, Labour MP for Hull West, both of whom supported women priests, said they were unhappy with the protection afforded to the minority. Adie sought to allay the anxiety by disclosing to the committee that the bishops were actively considering enshrining the Manchester statement in an Act of Synod – a device which, though not legally binding, has the moral force of the General Synod behind it. The hostile questioning continued during three further sessions in May. If the majority in the House of Bishops was already coming to the conclusion that an Act of Synod was essential, the mood of the ecclesiastical committee powerfully reinforced that view.

Carey was not required to appear before the committee until July

– after the House of Bishops had met to flesh out their January statement. The three-day meeting of the House in late June, this time in the Manchester business school, was an even more tense gathering than before. Carey and Habgood were convinced that the statement needed to be enshrined in an Act of Synod, but they were determined to resist traditionalist pressure to entrench it in law. The result of three days of tough negotiations was a complex package of measures which represented a significant extension of the January statement. Under the revised agreement, bishops who would neither ordain women nor delegate that responsibility to their suffragans could, as under the London plan, find a bishop from elsewhere (a commissary) who would ordain women on behalf of the Archbishop of their province (Canterbury or York). To cater for opponents of women priests who found themselves in dioceses where the bishop ordained women, the Church of England would be split into regions within which local traditionalist bishops would be nominated by colleagues to minister to dissenting parishes. As a back-up, the Archbishops of Canterbury and York would appoint no more than three suffragan 'flying bishops' to operate within their respective provinces. None of these bishops, however, would have automatic access to other dioceses; they were rather to be seen as ombudsmen whose job it was to monitor the effectiveness of the new arrangements. In a key passage, the statement also effectively ruled out the prospect of any of the traditionalist bishops invoking their rights under the legislation to bar women priests from their dioceses, exhorting them to demonstrate their goodwill by voluntarily renouncing their powers. Equally, the liberal bishops were pressed to show their goodwill by allowing traditionalist bishops access to their dioceses. This structure, the statement declared, would allow the co-existence of the 'two integrities'. Introducing the Act, Carey said it would 'help to offer reassurance to all without the complexity and delay which a supplementary Measure would involve.'

The final agreement represented a significant victory for the traditionalists – reflecting what one later described as a sea-change in the thinking of the bishops – and it won grudging approval in nearly all quarters. Among the liberal diocesan bishops only Baker, who was anyway soon to retire as Bishop of Salisbury, abstained. He argued that he could not accept that two views could co-exist. 'The Church has already decided to ordain women. We would be setting up two churches in one,' he said. Behind the closed doors of the meeting other bishops had also objected, but had been prevailed upon to toe the line. Carey said later that Baker's objections stemmed from a misunderstanding.

> None of us were actually saying that the two integrities were on a par, because once we ordain women we are actually saying, 'you are full priests. That is enshrined in the law and you are no different from men in that respect.' But the point about the second integrity is to allow the presence in the Church of England of those people, men and women, who believe this is a wrong decision.

MOW was so relieved that the traditionalist bishops had waived their rights to bar women priests from their dioceses that its initial reaction was positive. A spokeswoman said: 'It's unpleasant that women priests are still such a problem to a minority, but we're thankful there will be no no-go areas for us and there will be women priests in every diocese.' On reflection, however, MOW had second thoughts about the Act of Synod which, it felt, had been forced out of the bishops by the ecclesiastical committee. Its leadership was prepared to tolerate dissenters who doubted the validity of women priests or believed that the decision to ordain them had been wrong because the Church of England lacked the authority or because it was damaging to ecumenical relations. But, in a strongly-worded statement issued in September, it repeated Baker's call for a ban on the ordination of 'impossibilists' – those who denied that women could ever become priests. Dame Iris Murdoch, the philosopher and novelist, was one of nearly 500 signatories of a MOW advertisement calling on the General Synod to amend or reject the Act of Synod.

The traditionalist constituency, meanwhile, was split between those who felt they could trust the House of Bishops to protect them and those who did not. Broadhurst said the arrangements 'offered a way forward'. In reality, he and many others regarded them merely as a stop-gap solution, a 'breathing space' while they planned their futures. There were still traditionalists who hoped that the Archbishops would name prominent members of their constituency, like Austin or Broadhurst, as the 'flying bishops'; such figures, they believed, could yet provide a focus for the development of an alternative, orthodox Church within a Church. But the general mood was one of resignation; too many of the traditionalists were already giving up the fight and leaving. The climate of opinion in the Church seemed to be so dominated by the liberal view that they feared it was only a matter of time before their position was further eroded. Many of them were suffering from stress, and a few even had breakdowns. As one put it: 'We are now living in the gatehouse of a great mansion we once used to inhabit.'

With the Manchester agreement under his belt, Carey had less to fear when he and Habgood eventually appeared before the ecclesiastical committee on 5 July. The mood within the Church of England had changed; there was a buoyancy among the bishops who felt that they had successfully charted a course through very choppy waters. Though many traditionalists were still heading for the lifeboats, many others were hesitating. Carey told the committee that the bishops' envisaged the Act of Synod establishing the system of 'flying bishops' on a more or less permanent footing. More crucially, he reiterated that no traditionalist would be discriminated against when it came to promotions, though Habgood conceded that 'it would be difficult in the Church to have a leader who was actively rejecting those who had been ordained and saying they were not ordained at all.' Carey was also pressed on how the 'flying bishops' scheme would operate if a liberal bishop refused to allow a traditionalist parish to be visited by a traditionalist bishop from outside the diocese, but the question was never fully answered. Carey says now:

> The clergy would write to the provincial episcopal visitor or to me, saying my wretched bishop won't allow anyone to care for us. But the provincial visitor is my officer, my suffragan. I will then say to the bishop, Peter, or whoever, we've

committed ourselves to this arrangement in Manchester. I'm
sure you will allow Fred to come in and care for them, and I'll
get a short phonecall confirming it. I can't imagine there will
be any problems.

On the eve of the July meeting of the General Synod, which was to
hold a preliminary debate on the Act of Synod, the ecclesiastical
committee voted by 16 to 11 in favour of declaring the legislation on
women priests expedient, and by 17 to 10 in favour of the financial
provisions. Though many reservations had remained in the minds
of the minority, who wanted the Manchester statement entrenched
in a new Measure, the majority believed that the tide in favour of
women priests was now flowing 'too strongly to be resisted' without
alienating large numbers of people, both men and women. The
Synod had no difficulty 'taking note' of the Act of Synod; the real
test would come in December.

One group had been suffering largely in silence. Many conservative Evangelicals were opposed to women priests, but they had no
escape route to Rome. Instead, they began retreating into their
shells. In February 1993, a conference of conservative Evangelicals
called on the bishops to appoint more 'flying bishops' to cater for its
constituency, but the plea was ignored. Meanwhile, a group of
several hundred Evangelical clergy opposed to liberal develop-
ments in the Church of England – calling itself Reform – established a network of parishes which withheld part of their annual
financial quotas as a protest at the 'liberal agenda'. A number of
individual Anglo-Catholic parishes were also refusing to pay their
full share to the dioceses – a move regarded as subversive by the
bishops. This financial deprivation was certainly painful: the
Church Commissioners, the body which administers the Church of
England's finances and pays clergy salaries and pensions, had seen
£800m. wiped off its assets during the recession, and it was already
obliged to find compensation for those clergy who resigned over the
ordination of women priests, more than £1m. per 100 departing
clerics. In October, the conservative Evangelical Church Society
caused flutters at Lambeth Palace when it was unexpectedly given
permission by the High Court to challenge the Church of

England's legal right to ordain women. The challenge was based on the argument that the General Synod was exceeding its constitutional powers because it was altering fundamental doctrine. Dr David Samuel, the president of the Church Society, later resigned from the Church of England. The legislation sailed through both the House of Commons (215 for to 21 against) and the House of Lords (135 for to 25 against) and received the Royal Assent on 5 November. The following week the Act of Synod was approved by the General Synod after an hour-long debate, during which attempts by MOW and the liberals to emasculate it were thrown out. When it was passed, some of the militant pro-women campaigners in the public gallery muttered 'shame, shame' until they were ordered to leave the chamber by the chairman. The Synod was able to 'promulge the canons' – enshrining it in Church as well as secular law – at a special, one-day meeting in February, 1994. Some left the chamber in protest while a group of extreme Anglo-Catholics, led by Francis Bown, a Hull vicar, held a mock funeral for the Church of England in Dean's Yard. The stage was set for the Church of England to ordain its first women priests.

One question remained: how many Anglican clergymen would leave for Rome? On 19 November 1993, Hume finally produced detailed guidelines for easing the passage of the dissidents into the Roman Catholic Church. The terms were generous, but many believed they had taken too long in coming. In a statement agreed by the English Roman Catholic hierarchy at its November meeting, Hume reiterated the principle that Anglican congregations could be received in groups, led by their clergy, as long as they ultimately became integrated into the Roman Catholic community. Significantly, however, he added that these groups may be able to stay together for a lengthy period after their reception to provide mutual support. Even more crucially, the statement overcame two hurdles which had been facing Anglican clergy who wanted a 'fast track' route to Roman Catholic priesthood. It acknowledged that their Anglican ministries may well have been valid and it also envisaged married convert clergy (though confusion remains over whether their cases can be dealt with in this country or have to be referred to Rome). The guidelines were finally approved by the

Vatican in early December after Hume and a delegation of bishops had flown to Rome for an audience with the Pope. Hume later told friends that when he was shown in to see the 'head', the Pope had risen from his chair and said: 'Basil, Basil, be generous, be generous.' The Cardinal was then ushered in to see the 'deputy head', Ratzinger, who told him: 'Be flexible, be flexible.' 'So', Hume concluded, 'I went out and had a Campari.'

The Anglo-Catholics were delighted. Christopher Colven predicted that between 1,000 and 2,000 Anglican clergymen, many married with families, would transfer to the Roman Catholic Church over the next decade. 'The Vatican statement is a watershed and a very exciting moment. It is also a time bomb,' he said. More realistic estimates put the figures at 500 to 1,000. A further impetus was provided when the two Archbishops announced in February 1994 the names of the archdeacons they had chosen to be the 'flying bishops'. Only two, rather than the maximum of three, were appointed in February and neither of the two men – the Ven. John Gaisford, who became suffragan Bishop of Beverley, and the Ven. John Richards, who became suffragan Bishop of Ebbsfleet, Kent – were prominent members of the traditionalist constituency. Moreover, they were both relatively close to retirement. On 24 February, five Church of England bishops and 570 clergy signed a declaration, organized by Forward in Faith, accepting the full authority of the Roman Catholic Church, including the infallibility of the Pope. By August, more than 300 clergy had left the Church of England for Rome, 153 of whom had applied for compensation (at an estimated cost to the Church Commissioners of over £3m. by the end of 1995, though some will be clawed back in savings on stipends). Half a dozen congregations – from Kent to Fulham in London – had been received as groups, and as many more were in the wings. Geldard and a 30-strong group from his parish in Kent expect to move early next year. Dozens of Anglicans, both clergy and lay, have been received individually or with their families. Gummer was received at a discreet ceremony in Westminster Cathedral at the end of February, and Leonard – whose case was overseen by the Pope – became a Roman Catholic priest. Others, including the retired Bishop of Leicester, Richard Rutt, followed.

But there had been no high profile exodus; Hume's guidelines and an understanding with the Anglican bishops that the conversions should not be made in a mood of triumphalism conspired to keep the whole process unexpectedly *sotto voce*. Would-be converts were asked to keep their decisions private. But the mood among the traditionalists remains fluid. 'Most of my friends seem to be oscillating,' said one. 'One day they are going, the next they are staying.' Although senior Church leaders from the Anglican and Roman Catholic Churches continue the ARCIC discussions (the joint commission has just produced its response to the Vatican's questions over the ARCIC I report), they are a desultory, academic exercise. As if to ram the point home, the Pope issued a letter to all Roman Catholic bishops in June making clear that the Roman Catholic Church could never countenance the ordination of women priests, saying it lacked the authority to do so. His letter, which a future liberal Pope would find difficult to countermand, was vigorously criticized by Carey, who called on Rome to clarify 'how it sees the future of the ecumenical endeavour'.

Appropriately, it was the Bishop of Bristol, Barry Rogerson, who won the unofficial race among the bishops to ordain the first batch of the 1,200 women who were to become priests over the next few months. Carey had deliberately avoided going first, fearing that to do so would provoke dissent, so history was made in Bristol Cathedral on Saturday, 12 March 1994. Teams of vergers equipped with waikie-talkies patrolled the congregation on the look-out for trouble makers, but there were none. In an atmosphere of sheer elation, thirty-two women realized their dreams: as they were ordained by Rogerson, spontaneous applause echoed around the Cathedral's gothic arches for more than a minute. The newly-ordained women, many in tears, hugged friends and relatives in the congregation and mingled with the male clergy – on equal terms for the first time. In his sermon, Rogerson said the journey of these women 'has not been a journey of the mind or the head, but is seen by those they have touched and who know that the spirit of God is at work in them.' The following morning – Mothering Sunday – the women priests celebrated Communion for the first time, quietly beginning their new ministries. Similar scenes were replicated in cathedrals up and down the country in the following months. On 8 May, in Canterbury Cathedral, Carey told the 22 women he was about to ordain that they should rise above the hurt and try to help traditionalists 'pass through the imagination barrier'. Later that month, in Southwark Cathedral, Elsie Baker, whose parishioners in Blackheath had petitioned for her ordination to the priesthood 20 years earlier, was ordained a priest at the age of 80. The only real dissention surfaced, predictably, in the diocese of London: in one of the two ordination services in St Paul's Cathedral, a London vicar, Paul Williamson, who had unsuccessfully attempted to prevent the ordination of women in the courts, was allowed to intervene briefly to voice his protest that women priests were heretical. As he stood on the steps of the altar delivering his oration, male clergy who had come to support the women deacons attempted to cut him short by waving their orders of service and muttering 'time'; his protest was then succinctly dismissed by the registrar of the diocese. Hope sat at the far end of the Sanctuary, present but taking no part in the proceedings. After the service, as the newly-ordained women priests posed on the steps of the Cathedral for the press and delight-edly hugged their friends and relations, disillusioned traditionalists moped inside. 'It doesn't feel like Anglicanism any more,' complained one, who had swopped his dog collar for an open-necked shirt. 'It might as well be the United Reformed Church.'

What is the result of this revolution? On the surface, little has changed. There has been no sudden upsurge in the numbers of young people, women or men, who have been so enthused by the reforms that they are clammering to be ordained; the women who really yearned for the priesthood were already working in the Church and had been for years. In fact, in 1993, there was actually a sharp drop in the numbers being recommended for training. But there has been no massive exodus of traditionalist clergy either; the departures have constituted a trickle rather than a flood. More than a fifth of the clergy, their ambitions thwarted, will resentfully sit out their time in the Church of England, unable to recognize a tenth of their fellow clergy because of their gender. Schism is a fact; though there are no 'no-go' dioceses for women priests, there are hundreds of 'no-go' parishes. The liberal Protestant wing of the Church, meanwhile, will seize the opportunity to press its agenda, not so much because the issue of women priests has been a Trojan horse for liberal causes but because its natural opposition has now retired hurt, leaving the field clear: the Anglo-Catholic and conservative Evangelical power base in the General Synod has been decimated. Though MOW has been disbanded, a new campaign for the consecration of women bishops is already underway. It will encounter little resistance.

At the international level, schism is even more apparent. While 17 of the 30 provinces have now ordained women or said that they will, a handful of them, including Papua New Guinea and Central Africa, have given a resounding 'no'. Others are in transition; the governing body of the Church in Wales surprised everyone in April when it threw out legislation to ordain women. Some of these splits are likely to remain permanent symbols of division. A new, international theological commission designed to identify and resolve potentially destructive issues such as lay presidency (the Evangelical notion that lay people should be allowed to celebrate Communion), sexual ethics and inclusive language in the liturgy has replaced the Eames commission. But the central problem, that of the lack of any definitive source of authority in the Anglican Communion, is unresolvable. The gap between the conservative provinces and the progressive ones is liable to become so wide that the two groups will seem to be in different denominations. The 1998 Lambeth conference could prove a strained, and strange, affair.

The long-term health of the Church of England remains in doubt. Like a patient recovering from a major operation, it is still in shock, and it will be some time before anyone can assess the effects of the surgery. The Church's admission of women to the priesthood was probably inevitable; given its democratic structures, it could hardly have resisted the pressures of secular society indefinitely. But the hopes of many of the supporters of women priests that the dissent would melt away once the legislation had been passed have failed to materialize. Instead, in the spirit of compassion and tolerance, the bishops have been forced to buy peace at the cost of compromise and theological contortion. Many predicted that one of the main benefits of the ordination of women would be a renewed burst of energy as the Church suddenly found it could speak to the modern world with a single, coherent voice, confident that its own structures encapsulated the best values of a largely sceptical society. Instead, the internal bickering and dissension continue. But the alternative could have been far worse; if the legislation had failed and women had been forced to wait for another decade, the internal tensions could have been even more damaging. Meanwhile, no one yet knows how the long-term influence of women priests – and ultimately women bishops – will modify the power structures and thinking within the Church. Most hope they will nourish its very roots. 'Women have been given their integrity,' says Katharine Rumens, who was ordained as a priest on 30 April 1994 in Chelmsford Cathedral. 'We are a people reformed, remade and renewed. At last my job is complete and it makes sense to me. In fact, it all seems very normal now – the heavens haven't been rent open. I look to the future with great excitement.'